Sean
Shahriar!

Best 2009!

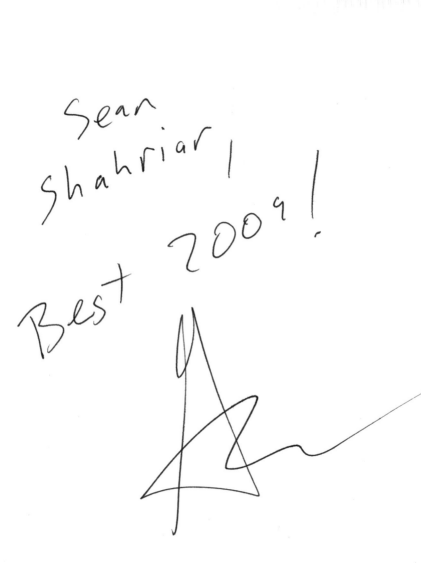

# The Dream

*How I Learned the
Risks and Rewards
of Entrepreneurship
and Made Millions*

Gurbaksh Chahal

THE DREAM
Copyright © Gurbaksh Chahal, 2008.
All rights reserved.

First published in 2008 by PALGRAVE MACMILLAN® in the
United States—a division of St. Martin's Press LLC, 175 Fifth
Avenue, New York, NY 10010.

Where this book is distributed in the UK, Europe and the rest of
the world, this is by Palgrave Macmillan, a division of Macmillan
Publishers Limited, registered in England, company number
785998, of Houndmills, Basingstoke, Hampshire RG21 6XS.

Palgrave Macmillan is the global academic imprint of the above
companies and has companies and representatives throughout
the world.

Palgrave® and Macmillan® are registered trademarks in the
United States, the United Kingdom, Europe and other countries.

ISBN-13: 978-0-230-61095-8
ISBN-10: 0-230-61095-1

Library of Congress Cataloging-in-Publication Data
Chahal, Gurbaksh.
    The dream : how I learned the risks and rewards of
entrepreneurship and made millions / Gurbaksh Chahal.
        p.   cm.
    Includes index.
    ISBN-13: 978-0-230-61095-8
    ISBN-10: 0-230-61095-1
    1. Success in business. 2. Entrepreneurship. 3. Internet
advertising. 4. Market segmentation. I. Title.
HF5386.C466   2009
338'.04092—dc22

                                                    2008040123

A catalogue record of the book is available from the British
Library.

Design by Letra Libre.

First edition: November 2008
10   9   8   7   6   5   4   3   2   1

*This book is for my father,*
*who taught me the importance of perseverance;*

*for my mother and grandmother,*
*who showed me the true meaning of love;*

*and for my three siblings,*
*who have been there for me every step of the way.*

# Contents

# Acknowledgments

I would like to thank, first and foremost, my brother Taj, who was there when it all began; my sisters, Nirmal and Kamal, whose love and support have always meant the world to me; my agent, Mel Berger, my publisher, Airié Stuart, and my co-writer, Pablo Fenjves, who subjected me to the most humbling and best therapy session of my life; and of course God, for giving me the willpower to reach my dreams so early in life.

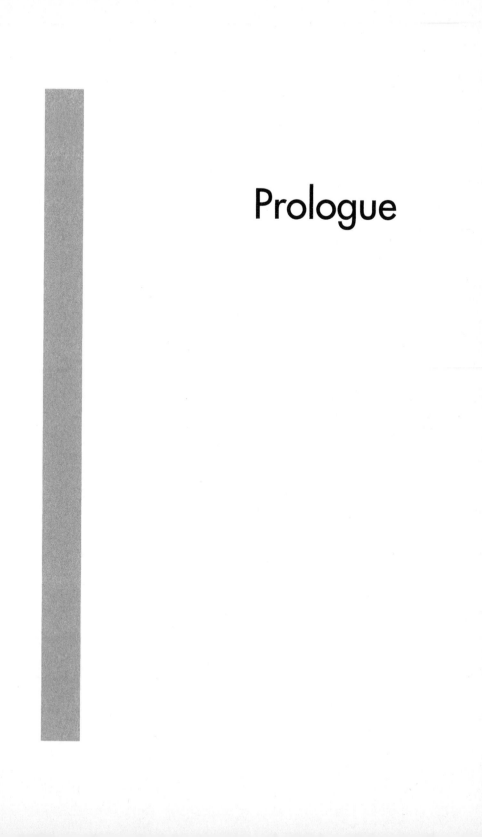

# Prologue

**W**hen I was sixteen years old I started a company in my bedroom, and within a few months I knew exactly what I wanted to do with my life: I would become an entrepreneur. There was one thing standing in my way, however: school. If I was going to pursue my goal, I would have to do it full time, and I needed my father's permission to drop out. This *wasn't going to be easy. More than a decade earlier, my family had come to America from India, settling in a one-bedroom apartment in a marginal section of San Jose, California. My father had arrived with $25 in his pocket, but his heart was full of dreams. "Education, education, education!" he would say, repeating it as if it were a mantra. "Education is the key that opens all the locks to all the doors in the world. My four children will become doctors and engineers. Maybe even both!"*

*I realized I couldn't bear another day of school, and I was ready to take the biggest risk of my life. It was the defining moment that every entrepreneur eventually faces in one form or another. I had to have* The Talk *with my father. I was terrified about approaching him. He was a man who valued education above almost everything else. How could I tell him I wanted to drop out of high school? Then again, if I was to pursue my dreams, how could I not?*

*Finally, one night after dinner, I braced myself and plunged in. "Dad, there's something we need to talk about," I said. I had a hard time meeting his eyes, so I focused on his turban.*

*"What?" he snapped.*

*"You know that stuff I've been doing in my room?"*

*"No," he said. "Not really."*

*"Well, it's turning out pretty well."*

*"As long as it's not interfering with school," he said.*

*Man, was I in trouble. But I felt compelled to press on.*

*"Take a look at this," I said.*

*Hesitantly I showed him my bank statement—the balance had edged north of $100,000. My father's hand flew to his chest, like a man on the verge of a heart attack. "W-what is this? W-where did you get all this money?" He turned toward the kitchen and hollered for my mother. "Gurbaksh is going to jail!"*

*My mother came running from the kitchen, eyes wide with alarm. "What did you say? To jail? Who is going to jail?"*

*"No one is going to jail!" I said.*

*When they were somewhat calmer, I proceeded to explain how I'd spent the past six months studying the dot-com market, watching young companies grow very rich, very quickly, and trying to figure out how they did it. One of them, DoubleClick, had piqued my interest, primarily because it was among the first companies to put advertising on the World Wide Web. People were spending more and more time on the Internet and less time reading newspapers and magazines or parked in front of their television sets, and traditional advertising was rapidly losing ground. The Web was fast becoming the next big sales tool.*

*But my parents weren't really listening. "I had hoped you would become a doctor," my father said, looking at me balefully.*

*"Dad, this is better. I promise."*

*Two days later, my father agreed to drive me to school to talk to the principal, and I was so grateful that I was near tears, but we*

*Chabals are not emotional men, so I simply thanked him for believing in me.*

*"I believe in you because I can see you believe in yourself," he said. "And obviously you're doing something right."*

*"I won't let you down," I said.*

*"You better not," he said. "Because I'm giving you exactly one year to prove yourself."*

*"One year?"*

*"Yes. One year. If this Internet business doesn't work out, you're going right back to school."*

*When we reached the campus, we parked and I led my father to the principal's office. He got to the point without wasting any time. "My son is dropping out," he said.*

*"Why?"*

*"He has never liked school. He is going to do bigger things."*

*By midsummer, after barely six months in business, I was posting revenues of $300,000 per month. And two years later, shortly after my eighteenth birthday—in what turned out to be one of the very first things I did as an adult—I sold my company for $40 million.*

*That was only the beginning.*

# An Immigrant Family

1

I was born in Tarn Taran, near Amritsar, in Punjab, India, on July 17, 1982, the youngest of four children, into a traditional Sikh family. My father studied hard and went to college, hoping to become an engineer, but when he graduated he couldn't find a satisfying job and joined the police academy. He and my mother met in 1971, a match arranged by their families, and were married that same year. She was a nurse and enjoyed a modicum of independence, but in most ways she was a traditional Indian woman. She had been taught that life revolves around the head of the household, the man, and she believed this to her core. When my father made a decision, she followed it without question. I would later find myself struck by this because her own family had actually pushed her to become independent, which in India—for people of a certain class—can only mean one of two careers: medicine or engineering. My mother wasn't interested in engineering, and she didn't think she had the patience or the stamina to become a doctor, so she settled for nursing, and she continued to work after she was married. In reality, though, after marriage her life was no longer her own. From that day forth, she did as she was told.

"It is the way it is," my mother often said.

In 1973, a year after they were married, my parents had their first child, a daughter, Kamal. Two years later, they had another daughter, Nirmal. This was a blow. In India, families want sons. A son is a potential breadwinner. And a son carries the family name and legacy into the future.

At this point, my parents decided to put their future in God's hands, and they both became exceedingly spiritual. They made frequent trips to the *gurdwara*, a Sikh temple, asking for a son, and they even prayed together at home.

*Gurbaksh (left) in India with his grandmother and brother Taj.*

Finally, late in 1978, my mother became pregnant again, and the following year they had a son, my brother, Taj. This was one of the greatest moments of their lives. God had listened to their prayers. They had a son! They were ecstatic.

Then they decided to try again. They thought the family would feel more balanced with two girls and two boys. They knew that perhaps they were being a little greedy, but the heart wants what it wants.

Again they went off to various *gurdwaras* to pray, and again they prayed at home. Again they gave God time to consider their request, and again their prayers were answered. When I came along in 1982, they named me Gurbaksh, which in Punjabi means "a gift from God."

Gift or not, those were unstable times in India. On June 3, 1984, two years after I came along, a group of separatists, looking to create an autonomous Sikh state within India's borders, demonstrated at the Golden Temple, the holiest of Sikh shrines. Indira Gandhi, the prime minister, ordered the army to clear the site, and there were many casualties—most of them Sikhs. To this day, the action is considered an unprecedented political disaster in modern Indian history.

My father had often talked about leaving India, and this incident convinced him that he should double his efforts. Like many Indians, he had his sights set on America, and he began to talk incessantly about leaving. There is no future for a Sikh in India, he would tell anyone who would listen. The country is corrupt. Opportunities are dwindling by the day. He wanted a better life, if not for himself then for his four children, and he believed that that life existed in America.

In 1984, my father applied for a visa through a U.S.-sponsored lottery system and received good news within months: The family's papers had been reviewed, and they could emigrate to the United States as soon as they wished. (This was partly because my mother was a nurse; then and now, there was a shortage of nurses in the United States.) My parents were thrilled, of course. They would move to California, where they had a few friends, and they would send for us within a year. My grandmother would stay behind with my two sisters, my brother, and me.

After fifteen hours in the air, the plane landed in San Francisco and my parents were met by a friend at the airport. He drove them to his home in Yuba City, a farming community about 125 miles to the north. They could have taken jobs picking peaches, but since they were both educated people they held out for something more.

Not long after, they moved to San Jose, a bustling, melting pot of a city, and for the next few weeks, as they looked for an apartment of their own, they traveled from the home of one acquaintance to the next. They had arrived with only $25 dollars to their names, having left the bulk of their savings behind with my grandmother—to feed and care for us kids—so things were more than a little tight.

It turned into an especially difficult first year for my parents. My father had a tough time finding a job. As a Sikh, he wore a turban and a full beard, and—despite his flawless English—many westerners were put off by his appearance. Eventually, though, he found work as a security guard, for $3.35 an hour—the minimum wage at the time—and my mother found a job as a nurse's aide (a step down from the work she had done in India, where she'd been director of nursing at a major city hospital). In due course they saved enough to make the deposit on a one-bedroom apartment on the gang-ridden east side of San Jose: first month, last month, and a security deposit.

In June 1986, my mother finally flew back to India to fetch us, and within days we were on our way to America: Kamal, Nirmal, Taj, my paternal grandmother, my mother, and me. I was a month shy of four at the time, so I don't remember much about the trip or about that first year, but before long I began to adapt to life in the New World.

On weekday mornings, when my parents went off to work and the older kids left for school, I stayed behind with my grandmother, Surjit Kaur. Having spent much of her lifetime in the field, picking red peppers and chilies to support herself and her only son, a one-bedroom apartment in America was nothing to complain about—despite the fact that she was afraid to venture beyond the front door.

Every morning, after the house emptied out, she would park me in front of the TV, where I watched *Barney* and other similarly hypnotic shows. Then I'd wander into the kitchen to watch her cook—she prepared Indian food every day since it was all she knew—and before long my siblings would drift home from school, often in tears. My oldest sister, Kamal, had just turned thirteen, an awkward age under any circumstances, but particularly difficult for a recent immigrant. To the other kids, she and Nirmal were *Fobs* or *Fobbies*—Fresh Off the Boat—and they were ridiculed endlessly. My brother, Taj, was subjected to much of the same. A quiet, unobtrusive boy, he was not fond of attention, but it was hard to hide under the *patka* he'd been wearing since age five. "The other children call me towel-head," he complained to my father.

"Don't listen," came the reply.

By the time I was sent to kindergarten, I had a vague idea of what I could expect, and I was terrified. Unfortunately, my fears were immediately confirmed. The class was full of Latinos, blacks, Asians, and a scattering of whites, but no Indians, so I was the one, true outsider. *Turban-head! Conehead! Papa Smurf!* And that was only the beginning.

"They call me Gandhi!" I told my father, wailing.

"So what? Gandhi was a great man. You should be proud."

"Nobody wants to be my friend!"

"Why would you want to be friends with children who call you names? You don't need such friends. You have your family."

"I don't want to go to school!"

"What? Not go to school! You are here to study, boy, and that's what you will do! And I expect good grades from you—the best!"

"But—"

"That's it! There will be no more talk on the subject."

Two or three times a week, I'd come home with my turban in my hand, and my hair, uncut since birth, spilling onto my shoulders. My father told me to ignore the other kids, assuring me that it would stop, but he was wrong. The kids in my class were relentless.

My grandmother was never less than sympathetic, though. "Everything is going to be okay," she would tell me. "Maybe things are a little bad now, but in my heart I know they will get better, especially for a smart boy like you." That was enough for me. I believed her, and that gave me strength.

My father had no time for petty annoyances. On the contrary, he never tired of reminding us that we were a most fortunate family. Sometimes he went a little overboard. If it was a particularly nice day, for example, he might point it out. "How about this great weather?" he'd say. "In India, you go through nine months of heat and then two months of monsoons. But look at us. We live in California."

And more: "Look how quickly things change in America! When I first got here, I was working as a security guard, but now I have a job with a company that manufactures hard drives for computers. People in this country are willing to take a chance on people like us."

We shopped at the local Goodwill store, McFrugal's, and at the Dollar Store, which was my favorite. Everything was a dollar. You could get shirts for a dollar. Shoes for a dollar. Three pairs of socks for a dollar. I actually looked forward to shopping there, because it was such a bargain. To this day, I like a good bargain. I learned at an early age that most people are very unwise about the way they spend their money, and I was determined not to be one of them.

I loved grocery shopping, too, because the stores were so colorful, and mostly because Mom always splurged on Twinkies. Shopping, for me, was almost a form of entertainment. I was out in the world, looking at stuff, seeing people, and I got a real kick out of using coupons to get good deals. I remember sitting at the kitchen table with my mother, helping clip coupons. We *loved* coupons, and I especially loved the ones for Little Caesars pizza. They would come with the mail every week or two, and I would look for them as if they were the prize in a box of Cracker Jack. For $5, you could get an extra-large pizza with two toppings, but the deal was only good on Mondays. So guess what we usually ate on Mondays? Two large pepperoni pizzas. That was some deal! Monday night became Family Pizza Night at the Chahals, and everyone loved it—even my grandmother.

"See how lucky you are?" my father would say. "Ordering in is a luxury."

*Gurbaksh at age seven with his sister Nirmal, at their apartment in San Jose.*

We were poor, and my parents were struggling, but everything about America was already a dream come true.

Not for me though: On the first day of fourth grade, for example, I arrived at school in bright yellow slacks, a bright yellow shirt, and a matching yellow turban that my mother had made with her own hands. The children couldn't stop staring, and even the teacher was curious. "Is it a special day for you people?" she asked.

I tried to bite my tongue, but I couldn't manage it. "No! It is not a special day! It is a *regular* day!"

"Well, thank you for clearing that up for us, Gurbaksh," she said with a harsh edge.

Since both my parents worked double shifts, Kamal became a second mother to me. She helped me with my homework and went to PTA meetings on my parents' behalf, sharing what she'd learned from my teachers as soon as Mom and Dad got home from work. "He's doing well. He's getting mostly Bs. But he's smart and he could get As if he applied himself."

"So you're not applying yourself?" my father would say.

Kamal went on: "He doesn't speak up in class. And he mumbles when he speaks and won't look people in the eye."

"I'm shy," I protested.

"And he's not very social," Kamal went on. "He should make more of an effort to make friends."

"Everybody hates me," I said.

"Stop whining," my father would say, and then he would launch into one of his regular tirades. "You children are such ingrates! Do you have any idea how much your mother and I have sacrificed to give you this opportunity? Not another word out of you! Now sit down and do your homework!"

Eventually I did stop whining, mostly because it didn't do any good. My parents were too busy making their way in the New World to worry about my little problems. And they did have problems of their own: One Saturday I heard a scream, and I rushed into the living room to find my father flat on his back on the floor, with my mother, still screaming, on her knees next to him, still screaming, and my sister on the phone, calling for help. I was only nine at the time, but I noticed the way my father's eyes kept darting around the room without really seeing us, and I remember thinking, *He is looking at Death. He is fighting with Death.*

By this time we were all crying, and by the time the ambulance arrived we were near despair. But they stabilized him on the way to the hospital, where he spent the next three days hooked to all manner of pinging, bleating monitoring equipment. He had had a pretty serious heart attack, and the doctors told my mother that he was lucky to be alive.

When my father finally came home, we tiptoed around him, as if he were fragile, and at every opportunity we told him how glad we were to have him back. None of us had ever had a warm, fuzzy relationship with Dad, but we certainly loved him, and for a long time afterward I loved him more ferociously than ever.

Months later, when he was finally beginning to feel somewhat recovered, the technology sector took a dive and he was laid off. "I will find something," he said. "Not to worry. One must always have a positive attitude."

A few weeks later, my father got a job with the postal service. The money wasn't particularly good, but they had excellent health benefits, along with a solid retirement plan, and he began thinking about moving the family into a nicer neighborhood. He announced his intentions one Sunday afternoon, just before we went to the video store for Bollywood Movie Night. "We are going to be extra careful with our money from now on," he said. "We need to save up for our new home." We all cheered, as if the new home were already ours, then we piled into the car for the drive to the video store.

Sunday night was my favorite night of the week. My father would walk into the store. He always said the same thing to the clerk. "We are looking for a family movie. Do you understand me? A *family* movie."

"Yes sir, I understand precisely."

We would then go home and take our regular seats in front of the TV, and within minutes we would be glued to the unfolding stories. The movies were always very chaste, because Bollywood actors aren't even permitted to kiss. Sometimes they would look at each other with intense longing, however, and you knew that at any moment they would leap into each other's arms, but the director always cut away at that point. The next scene was usually some kind of frenzied dance number that took the place of the kissing and whatever followed.

My father would get very worked up about those scenes. When the actors began to look at each other with longing, he'd hunt around for the remote. "Where's the remote? Give me the remote! I told that silly clerk I wanted a *family* movie, and he gives me this immoral trash!"

Invariably, we'd arrive at the song-and-dance number before Dad found the remote, and he'd sit back and relax a little, but he was never less than vigilant. And we could expect to see him tense up at least two or three more times in the course of the film. "Where's the remote? Who is hiding the remote?"

Poor Kamal always got a little nervous at these junctures. Some years earlier, my father had attempted to fast-forward through a racy scene, and the remote had gone dead in his hands. He had become quite upset, and had turned to look at Kamal. "You are the eldest child," he said, unable to hide his displeasure. "You will make sure that nothing like this ever happens again."

Every Sunday, we would go back to the store to return the video, and to find another one, less racy, perhaps, and my father always let the poor clerk have it. "I said I was looking for a *family* movie! What is wrong with you! They almost *kissed!*"

In 1992, the years of frugality finally paid off. My parents felt secure enough to take their savings and buy a small house on Gridley Street, on the east side of San Jose. We were still in the heart of the projects, but this was an actual home, and it even had a small yard.

It was almost directly across the street from the McCollam Elementary School, and one afternoon—thinking I should try to start losing some of that Twinkie-fueled weight—I went over to the school's rundown basketball courts, empty at that hour, and started shooting hoops. Before long, I noticed a pair of Hispanic teenagers watching me. I tried to ignore them.

"Hey!" one of them said.

I kept shooting.

"Hey! Towel-head! I'm talking to you! What the hell are you doing, man?"

"Excuse me?" I said.

"You heard me," he said.

"I'm shooting baskets," I said.

They came closer. "Take that thing off your head," the guy said. The other one said nothing, and for a moment I wondered whether he was mute.

"I can't," I said. "It's part of my religion."

"You don't listen too good, do you?" he said, and he took a knife out of his pocket. "Take that shit off right now!"

I dropped the basketball and began the slow, laborious process of removing the many hooks that were holding my turban together. I was on the verge of tears, but I forced myself not to cry. When I was done, I handed him the turban, hardly breathing, and he and his friend called me an ugly name and walked away. As soon as they were out of sight, I picked up the basketball and ran home, and I was sobbing by the time I came through the front door. My grandmother hurried out to see what was wrong and was shocked to find me standing there in tears, without my turban.

I told her what had happened, crying even harder now, and she took me in her arms and held me close. "But it's not your fault, Gurbaksh," she said. "You did nothing wrong."

"I know," I said.

"Even so," she continued. "I don't want you going over there by yourself anymore. Do you understand?"

"Yes," I said. But I didn't. Not really.

When my father came home, I repeated the story.

"And you just gave them your turban?" he asked.

"One of them had a knife," I said. "I thought he was going to cut me."

"Well, I'm glad that nothing happened, but next time you need to be stronger. You need to stand up to people like that."

I had gone to my father to be comforted, but his response only made me feel worse. And it was doubly painful because I wished I *had* stood up to those two boys. I had wanted to tell them, just as I'd wanted to tell everyone who had ever taunted me, that I was proud of my family, proud of my heritage, and proud to be a Sikh—but I was just a kid, and I didn't know where to begin. Instead, I began to long for another kind of existence, one where I was in charge.

That same year, my brother Taj turned thirteen, and he had a formal turban ceremony at our home, with a Sikh priest in attendance. I was ten at the time, and both Taj and I were wearing *keski*- or *patka*-style turbans, the turban of choice for children. Our hair was braided and tied into a single, bulblike knot atop our heads. Now it was time for Taj to make the transition to a *dastar*-style turban, the peaked turban one sees on most adult males.

I guess in some ways the ceremony is the Sikh equivalent of a bar mitzvah. I wasn't thrilled because I knew I would be next, and I didn't like the idea of someday being forced to endure the same ritual. I had already suffered enough ridicule with my little *patka*, and I knew that a full, adult turban would only make things worse. I was tired of being picked on for being different. I wanted to blend in, to avoid notice, to disappear.

I think I half hoped that my brother would refuse to have anything to do with the ceremony, because I knew my turn was just around the corner. There was a great deal of talk during the service about the turban's significance, which has been an important part of Sikh culture since the time of Guru Nanak, who founded the religion five hundred years ago. The turban is part of the Sikh identity and speaks to our spirituality, honor, self-respect, moral values, courage, and piety. Leaving our hair uncut, and tying the turban daily, is a token of our love for and our obedience to the Sikh gurus. At age ten, I can't say I fully understood much of this, but I sat through the ceremony with only moderate fidgeting, and when it was over, *finally*, I was among the first in line for food.

That night, when we got home, my father continued to talk about the ceremony. Clearly, he had been very moved by the proceedings. His own father-in-law had been a priest at a Sikh temple in India, and my father had brought the religion and the culture with him to America. We went to local services on Wednesdays and Sundays, and after the Sunday services, I had Sunday school. We also had morning prayers every morning, the Japji Sahib, which my father recited in *Gurmukhi*, which literally means "from the mouth of the guru." Although I had no idea what the words meant, I was urged to memorize them, and I was quite proud of the accomplishment.

My father tried to explain it to me, as he explained other aspects of the Sikh religion over the years, and only a little of it stuck. I knew, for example, that Sikhs believed in a universal God and that they followed the teachings of the ten gurus, or "ambassadors." I also knew that the religion had its roots in Hinduism and that—like most religions—it was focused on the idea of salvation. And I was familiar with the idea of karma, and of reincarnation, and with the fact that Sikhs viewed life as a cycle of birth and rebirth that stopped only when one was united with God.

The summer after the turban ceremony, my father took me to India to acquaint me with my past. "I want to make sure that you never forget where you came from," he said.

"Okay," I said. I didn't have the heart to tell him that I remembered absolutely nothing. I would always feel tied to my culture, and proud of it, but I felt more American every day.

We first went to Chandigarh, to meet a large contingent of cousins on my mother's side, and I can say unequivocally that I felt absolutely no connection to them. They weren't particularly welcoming, and within days the visit had turned into some kind of competition. I was the dumb American; they were the smart Indians. They were older than I, and they would show me their battered schoolbooks and ask me to do one of the problems—algebra, for example—and of course I wouldn't know where to begin. This would reduce them to paroxysms of laughter. "How stupid people get in America," they would say. "In America, you learn nothing."

My father took me aside and told me to ignore them. "They are just jealous," he said. "They wish they could live in America. But that's the way people are. If they can't have what you have, they will bring you down."

Before long, we left and went to visit my grandmother's sister in a tiny village in Uttar Pradesh. The place was incredibly primitive. There was no running water, and no electricity, and the outhouse seemed to be miles away, but the people here—family and nonfamily alike—welcomed us with open arms. There were smiles and warm embraces, and everyone seemed genuinely happy to see us.

It taught me a valuable lesson, which served me well years later, when I went into business, and the lesson is this:

> **Always surround yourself with people who want you to succeed. That seems simple on the surface, but when you get out there, in the real world, you will discover that most people are rooting for you to fail. Stay away from them.**

"Gurbaksh-Ji!" they called out. "Come here! Let me take a closer look at you, you handsome boy." This *Ji* is a term of endearment, and is pronounced like the letter G. (Years later, while I was still in my teens, people began calling me G, short for Gurbaksh, and the name stuck. That is how I'm known to this day.)

That first night, our hosts prepared a big meal for us, which included *bakra* (goat), a rare treat for people of such modest means, but they did it selflessly, with great joy. They had few material possessions, but their hearts were very full.

And they made us eat until *we* were very full. That's one of the more curious aspects of Indian hospitality, especially as it pertains to my parents' generation. Any time you go to someone's house, they insist on stuffing you to the point where it starts hurting. You don't eat until you're full; you eat until you're in pain. I'm sure some other cultures are similarly generous about food, but in India you run the risk of insulting your hosts if you don't eat, so you keep shoveling it in until you feel as if you'll explode.

"Everybody is nice to us here," I told my father during a private moment. "And there's so much food."

"This is why I brought you back to India," he said. "So you would know; so you would remember."

Later still, I found myself talking to one of my grandmother's cousins. "In this family, everything is about love," she said. "All we have is each other, and we cherish this gift, and we are always mindful of the need to be good to one another. People who have too much often lose sight of the things that really count."

I must tell you, I felt loved for every minute of our stay. If the day was hot, someone would appear at my side with a fan. If I even *looked* a little hungry, snacks would materialize at my side. And if I so much as yawned, people went out of their way to entertain me or to offer me a cool spot in which to take a nap. I felt like a young prince.

The thing that made the biggest impression on me, however, was what I'd been told about the need to appreciate one another. *All we have is each other.* There was no TV here. No video store. The only source of entertainment was a radio, in fact, and everyone enjoyed sitting in a room together listening to music and sharing stories. They were a family in the best sense of the word, and it was clear they loved each other's company.

That trip to India was the most extravagant vacation I had ever been on. All of our other vacations, as far as I can remember, consisted of a weeklong road trip in the early part of the summer. My father would rent a van, the seven of us would pile inside, and off we'd go. One year it was San Diego. Another, Los Angeles. And one summer we drove all the way to Vancouver, which took seventeen hours.

Years later, when I thought back to these summers, I realized that my father had made the effort to take us on vacation for a couple of reasons. The first is simple: He wanted to give us something special, something to remember, even if it was a bit of a financial hardship. And the second—the real lesson—is that he wanted to expose us to the world beyond our neighborhood. I believe he did this in the hope that perhaps someday we would reach for bigger things.

Also, no matter where we went, we always visited the local *gurdwara.* This gave the trip a religious component, and it also provided my father with an opportunity to remind us, again and again, that we were God-fearing people.

"Whatever you do, wherever you are," my father often said, "never forget that God is watching."

# A New CEO

In the fall of 1996, at the age of fourteen, I started freshman year of high school. I was a heavyset kid with a turban, and puberty had arrived way too early—so I had a pronounced mustache and beard. Whenever I looked in the mirror, I felt as if even my genes were betraying me.

The school was called Independence High, and—since my brother was a student there—I imagined I would show up on my very first day and be introduced to a great group of instant friends. That didn't happen, though, because Taj and his friends were four years older than me, and I didn't really exist for them. It was deeply disappointing. I was tired of being alone, tired of being the perpetual outsider, and I longed for human companionship. Alas, despite the large number of Indians at Independence High, I didn't feel any connection to any of them, or them to me. I didn't feel any connection to the Latinos, either, or to the Koreans, or to the Americans, black or white. It seemed as if everyone already had all the

*Gurbaksh on the cross country track team in high school, freshman year.*

friends they wanted and that I'd come to the party too late. School seemed to get worse for me with each passing year.

In 1997, the year before I launched my first company, a great many people in Silicon Valley were getting very rich, very fast. My father had become somewhat obsessed with the stock market, which piqued my own interest, and before long I was following the news as assiduously as he was. I was particularly curious about some of the fledgling Internet companies, many of which were located right there in San Jose and in neighboring Palo Alto. Everything I read about them excited me, even the many things I didn't understand. Still, I sensed that these entrepreneurs were riding a wave that was going to change the world, and I found myself longing to be part of it. That discovery made me hate school more than ever. I was a sophomore, a B+ student, with a 3.5 GPA, but that still didn't do it for me. I didn't know how I could possibly survive another three years of high school. I desperately wanted out.

In my eagerness to escape, I applied to an accelerated program at Accel Middle College, which had a program that offered college classes in a college setting and could lead to early graduation. The students were focused on academics, and nobody made fun of my turban or asked silly questions about "my people." Still, I didn't find it exactly inspiring. If school was supposed to prepare one for life, it didn't seem to be working for me. I wanted to start living, not endlessly preparing. What's more, all that preparation seemed like a waste of time. I am impatient by nature, and I wanted to make myself useful to my family. I was tired of watching my parents struggle. They were putting in fourteen-hour days just to get by—my father at the post office, my mother as an RN—and they hardly had time to enjoy the family. That, too, made me think: I had been taught that life was about balance, but their lives were completely without balance. They worked so hard that there was little time for anything else. It took me several years to learn that happiness is elusive without balance.

In the early evening, exhausted, my father would come home from his job at the post office, sit at the kitchen table, and— after perusing the business sections of various newspapers— park himself in front of the computer to study the stock market. Before long, he was actually making more money as a day trader than he was at his job. What's more, there was so much easy money around that he was buying stock on margin, which meant he was gambling with funds he didn't have. If he had $5,000 to invest, for example, he could buy $15,000 worth of stock. If the stock went up, he would make money on the full $15,000, turning a profit on shares he hadn't paid for. He thought this was wonderful and miraculous. It was what America was all about.

This is when I first heard about DoubleClick, a company that provided advertising services on the Internet. In the company's initial public offering (IPO), it was valued at $300 million, but at its peak, it was said to be worth $15 *billion* dollars. It was insane, but it was also very appealing, and the more closely I looked at DoubleClick's world—advertising— the more fascinating I found it.

I began to see that perception was reality. Many of the most successful companies were making no money whatsoever, but everyone assumed that the Internet was on the verge of exploding and that before long everyone would be rolling in cash. Some of these companies didn't even have rudimentary business plans, but they didn't seem to need them: They were successful simply because they were part of the dot-com boom, which in many respects was still largely illusory. Everyone was saying that the Internet was going to revolutionize the world—and, indeed, they were right—but many of those so-called cutting-edge companies had no idea what to do with themselves when the revolution finally came.

As any business person will tell you, the value of a traditional company is based on thirty times its EBITDA (earnings before income and tax depreciation of assets). If the company makes $1 million a year, it is said to be worth $30 million. But the Internet wasn't measured in those terms because most people weren't making any money. Instead, Internet companies were evaluated on the *perception* that someday, in the not-too-distant future, simply because of their connection to the Internet, they would be rolling in huge amounts of cash. It wasn't about their ideas. Or about the people who ran the companies. Or even about a vague business plan that might have sounded a little smarter than the next guy's business plan. It was all based on their association with a world no one fully understood but one that was poised to explode. That was the level of craziness back then. All you had to do was *look* like you knew something about the Internet, perhaps something other people might not know, and investors figured you would soon be rocking their world.

There was a lesson here, and it's an old one: If it's too good to be true, it probably is. Such a simple lesson, and yet so hard for so many of us to learn. And people *still* don't learn. Take the subprime mortgage mess. For three, four, maybe five years, borrowing money beyond our means seemed like a good deal, but if anyone had taken the time to think beyond that, they would have seen disaster looming. You didn't have to be a genius to figure that out; it boiled down to simple, common sense.

Every morning, early, my father and I would be parked in front of the television, bonding over the business news on

CNBC. The world seemed full of possibilities. I began to think about launching a venture of my own, of becoming a business-man. I watched the transformation in my father as he picked one winner after another, and I liked what I saw. As he watched the stock climb, he would break into a big, broad smile, until he was literally beaming. He was having a very good time. He was loosening up. He finally felt that he was getting ahead. *This* was why he had come to America, to make a life for his family.

Often I would help him with his decisions. If he was in-terested in a particular company, I would research it for him, and we would discuss the possibility of buying a few shares. He treated me like an equal, like his partner. Together we learned about buying on margin, about options trading, about puts and calls. Before long I found myself leaping out of bed at the crack of dawn, pouring myself a bowl of cereal, and parking myself in front of the television. I had the morning newspaper to my left and a pad and pencil to my right. The fact is, anyone can do this. It's just like homework, except it's the real world. It takes time and effort to get an A, and the same rules apply here, but the difference is that this is worth taking very, very seriously. After all, we're not talking about grades—we're talking about serious money.

When my father finally emerged from his bedroom, eyes still heavy with sleep, he would plunge in without small talk. "What's new this morning? What looks good?"

We studied charts together. Looked over annual reports. Discussed a company's earnings. I began to understand all the critical elements on which a company's performance was based, the same elements on which my debut company would soon be judged. It was strange. In ten years, I had gone from watching *Barney* to watching the business news, and I found the business news a lot more compelling.

As I've said, we are not overtly emotional men, my father and I, and we don't go in for that touchy-feely stuff, but this joint experience—the daily business talk, the morning briefings—created an atmosphere in which we could really bond.

"I like DoubleClick," I remember saying.

"What do they do?"

"Advertising," I said. "On the Internet."

But we didn't invest in DoubleClick. There were too many other options, and at times it seemed as if all of them were profitable—as if we could do no wrong.

At one point, emboldened by his modest successes, my father began to think about moving the family out of the 'hood. On weekends, he took us house hunting, until at long last we stumbled across a new development in a nice section of San Jose. At that point, the thirty houses hadn't progressed beyond the foundations, but five hundred people were already lined up to buy. The developer, clearly overwhelmed, resorted to a lottery system, and we were among the lucky ones. (Not the first time the Chahal family had struck gold with a lottery!) We were ecstatic. My father immediately wrote a check for the down payment, and on the ride home we talked about the size of the big-screen TV we'd be putting in the family room.

A few days later, my father got a call from a complete stranger. The man offered him $50,000 for the lot, but my father wouldn't sell. The home was more important to him. It was why he had come to America. "I'm not interested," he said. "This isn't about money. This is for my family."

On October 27, 1997, with our dream home already half completed, the market crashed. My father, never an emotional guy, fell apart completely. He had bought a lot of stock on margin and lost everything, plus he was about to lose money he didn't have.

That night, at the dinner table, he told us that the dream was no longer viable. We would not be moving into our new home. Worse, it looked as if the market was going to keep sliding. It had dropped 500 points, and he suspected there was worse to come. "In the morning, as soon as the market opens, I will sell everything," he said. "We will end up with nothing, but at least we won't be in debt."

The following morning, the minute the market opened, he sold everything. Half an hour later, the Dow climbed 324 points. My father was doubly crushed. If he had held on for another hour, he would have recouped most of his losses, and we would have been able to move into our new home. Now we would lose even the down payment.

That was the first time I had ever seen my father cry. Here was a man who always played his cards close to the vest, and he was sobbing in front of the entire family. He was defeated, and I was terrified for him.

"I am a complete failure," he said, tears streaming down his cheeks. "I have failed my family. I owe all of you an apology."

He left for work before any of us had a chance to comfort him.

A few days later, with no explanation whatsoever, my father snapped out of his depression. "One way or another, we are going to move into that new house," he said, and I remember being powerfully affected by the sudden change in attitude. That resilience and determination would forever be ingrained in my thinking, and the lesson was clear: *Never give up.*

In the weeks ahead, we did everything we could to raise money. Dad sold Mom's car and began chauffeuring her to and from work. Mom began taking double shifts at the hospital. Dad volunteered for overtime. We kept clipping coupons. We even sold the TV.

"We will go back to the way it used to be," my father said. "There will be belt-tightening for us all. Sacrifices must be made."

I had learned many lessons from this experience—all important. Specifically, I'd seen firsthand that moving on is often one of the hardest things to do in life. But it's critical. You will make mistakes, and you will get hurt, but you have better things to do than to wallow in self-pity. This is a very important lesson for anyone in business, so try to remember it when you get knocked down (because you *will* get knocked down).

All of us did what we could to help. I remember seeing a NOW HIRING sign at a local McDonald's, which was right across the street from the high school, and—because I loved their burgers and fries—I thought I'd be a perfect salesman: I really believed in the product.

School got out at three-thirty, and I figured I could work from four to eight, five days a week, and still get back to the house in time for dinner and homework. One day after school I went inside and filled out an application. The manager was there, so I asked if he would review it then. He emerged from the back office and took one look at me, and I knew immediately that a job wasn't in the cards. He couldn't stop staring at my turban, but he humored me and went through the motions. We sat in one of the empty booths. "What do you do?" he said, glancing at the application with little interest.

"I'm a student," I said. "I go to school across the street."

"How old are you?"

"Fifteen." In California, you can work at age fifteen if you get permission from your parents, and I knew that wasn't going to be a problem.

"What kind of work have you done in the past?"

"I haven't worked," I said. "But I help at home in the kitchen, and I can do anything. I'm a very fast learner." His eyes kept drifting to my turban. "Just give me a chance," I pleaded. "You won't regret it. I am doing this to help my family. I'm very responsible for a kid my age."

I couldn't sell myself, though. "I'm sorry," he said. "I just hired a bunch of people, but I have your number and I'll call if there's another opening."

For the rest of the year, I passed that McDonald's every day after school, and the NOW HIRING sign never came down. But I didn't go back in to reapply. I knew I could say "Would you like fries with that?" just as brightly and convincingly as the next person, but that's not what it was about. I was convinced it was about my appearance. It was about the turban. Maybe the manager didn't have an issue with it, but he probably assumed it would bother the customers, and he must have felt it wasn't worth the risk. Plus, where would I put my cute little McDonald's cap? Seriously, though, the rejection bothered me. I didn't want to be at the mercy of other people. I knew that someday I would be my own man, run my own show.

Meanwhile, both my sisters got part-time jobs and my brother found a cheap used bike and landed a newspaper delivery route. The family was in survival mode.

"Sacrifices must be made," my father kept saying, and he never got tired of showing us how it was done. This also proved to be a valuable lesson. I learned perseverance from him. I learned that the road to success is paved with failures. Most of all, as I've said, I learned that one should never, ever give up. Tough as things were, my father had pulled himself together. And he never got tired of reassuring us that we were going to be all right.

A month after the stock market crash, when the housing market began to pick up, we put a FOR SALE sign in front of our modest Gridley Street home. That was the only equity we had, and we needed it—badly.

In mid-January, we got a decent offer, and a month later we moved into our new digs. We rented a U-Haul truck and spent the entire weekend making trips to and from the house, and when we finally unloaded the last of the boxes I could see joy and victory in my father's eyes. He had managed to keep his word to his family. Despite the setbacks, he had given us a new home. It wasn't a palace by any stretch of the imagination, but it was a huge step up from the 'hood. There were five small bedrooms. I shared one of them with my brother, and my sisters took the one next door. My parents were in the room across the hall, my grandmother slept at the end of the corridor, in a small room that had its own bathroom, and the fifth room was our prayer room (Baba Ji's room). There was no fighting over this room: We all understood that under our father's roof, a space would always be set aside for worship.

That first night—with the kitchen still a long way from unpacked—we splurged on Kentucky Fried Chicken. We ate with our hands, grinning at each other across the table. We were happy. We were *home.*

The next day, before dinner, my father ran a brief *ardas* ceremony, in which we thanked God for his generosity. And over the next two weeks, we performed the *akhand* path, reading the entire Holy Book to give thanks, again, for our many blessings. The real ceremony usually takes place over the space of three days, and it is supposed to be performed, uninterrupted, by a team of professional readers, but my parents had jobs to go to and my siblings had school *and* jobs, so we spread it out over a longer period without suffering any ill effects.

So there we were, living the middle-class dream. My parents had made it. We had left the projects for a nice neighborhood. Things were looking good.

I, meanwhile, had become obsessed with CNBC, with making something of my life. I was driven. I wanted to be successful, and I wanted it to happen quickly. Inspired by the many entrepreneurs I kept seeing on the news, I decided I would build a company from the ground up, something that was wholly mine. I remained drawn to the Internet, which was still in its embryonic stages. Nowadays, of course, everyone knows what the Internet is, and life would be almost unimaginable without it, but back then, it was still uncharted territory. I was fascinated by the madness and euphoria that seemed to affect everyone connected to it.

In the fall of 1998, I finally got accepted into the accelerated program at Accel Middle College. When I did the math, I realized I could be a doctor by the time I was twenty-five, which of course would have been the fulfillment of my parents' dreams. But I had absolutely no interest in becoming a doctor—despite the fact that George Clooney made it look so cool on *ER*. My heart was in business.

Much as I disliked school, it was refreshing to be in an adult environment, among mature students who were thinking about their future.

The school hours were also a big plus. I had mandatory classes between twelve and two, Monday through Friday, but the rest of the time I was pretty much on my own. And I didn't have to attend any of the college courses as long as I did the required work and kept up my grades. I also used the opportunity to challenge myself. For example, I was a bit of an introvert, so I signed up for public speaking. On the first day of class, the professor launched right in. "I am going to hand out a list of topics, at random," she said. "Whatever topic you get, be prepared to come in and make a speech about it next week."

My topic was Viagra, which was new on the market. How was I going to talk about erectile dysfunction? This was an especially difficult topic for me, partly because I was a virgin and partly because the topic of sex—even chaste near-kisses in Bollywood movies—was completely taboo in our house. I couldn't go to my mother and say, "Well, you're a nurse, and there's this new drug on the market, and maybe you can help me out with my talk." And I couldn't discuss sex with my siblings because I suspected that they knew even less about the subject than I did.

I thought back to an incident some years earlier, back in the eighth grade, when one of the girls in my class phoned the house.

"Who was that girl?" my father asked, visibly angry. "What kind of girl calls a boy? What did she want from you?"

"She wanted to know what we had to read for homework," I said.

"That is unacceptable!" my father almost shouted.

On another occasion, a different girl called about another assignment, but I didn't hear about it till the following day, when she revealed that my father had told her angrily never to call the house again and abruptly hung up on her. "I'm sorry," I said. "He was napping. The phone must have startled him."

I'm not sure she believed me. My father was old-fashioned and rigid. He simply didn't understand. He came from another world, and the idea that his children might adapt to this new, "morally questionable" land must have terrified him. I was interested in women, of course. Very interested. But I didn't think they were interested in me.

At the end of the day, I realized I had to get through this class assignment without help, and I plunged in. I researched the subject in the library and on the Internet, and before long I had put together a coherent speech. I practiced at home, in front of the mirror, with the door locked: "Among the various causes . . . redirecting the flow of blood to the penis . . . the psychological implications . . ." and so on and so forth. On the big day, I got to my feet, made my way to the front of the class, and managed to get the nervous tremors under control. When my five-minute speech ended, right on time, the class applauded. I had been expecting a standing ovation, but I wasn't totally crushed. And the professor really liked it: She gave me an A.

I also took Philosophy 101. I was just a kid, but I was curious. What does life mean? What do the Great Thinkers say it means? What could I learn from them? I did a paper on Socrates, comparing his thinking to other philosophers of the time, and there are two quotes from him that I remember to this day. The first is: "Remember that there is nothing stable in human affairs; therefore avoid undue elation in prosperity, and undue depression in adversity." And the other one, on a lighter note: "By all means marry; if you get a good wife, you'll be happy. If you get a bad one, you'll become a philosopher."

*Gurbaksh at age sixteen, outside a classroom at Accel Middle College.*

I plugged along at Accel, though not with any great joy. Even here, most of my classes began to feel like a monumental waste of time, and I was eager to get on with my life. I wanted to do something in the world of Internet advertising, like that monolith DoubleClick, but I wasn't exactly sure how to go about it.

Meanwhile, I looked around for other business opportunities. I noticed, for example, that a lot of blue-chip companies had been slow about adapting to the Web, so I went out and bought a dozen domain names for twenty bucks apiece. The process was simplicity itself: I went online and registered names like Dell.net, HP.net, and so forth, then parked myself in front of the family computer and wrote emails to each of the companies, offering to sell them their own domain names for $10,000. This did not go over very well. Forty-eight hours later, I received a package from Federal Express, which my mother found more than a little disturbing. "You are just a boy," she said. "Who is sending you things by Federal Express?"

It was one of the companies I had contacted, and they weren't exactly thrilled by my so-called offer. The letter was basically a cease-and-desist order, and it included a request that I immediately surrender the domain name. The next day there were two more FedEx letters, from two other companies, and the language was almost identical. One of them talked about "trademark violations" and gave me only hours to make things right. I honestly hadn't known I'd been infringing on a trademark, and I immediately wrote the companies to let them know that they could have their names back, *for free*. "I am just a high school kid," I explained. "I didn't know what I was doing."

I had gone into that misguided little venture thinking I was going to be rich, but I hadn't done my homework. There is a big difference between trying to scoop up domain names for profit and infringing on a trademark—and I had done the latter. Somebody else, somebody smarter than I, had acquired the name "business.com," and he subsequently sold it for $7.5 million. But he had done his research. Nobody owned that name. I promised myself that there would be no shortcuts next time. If I had a job to do, no matter how small, I would always do it right.

One day I found myself at a local flea market, talking to a guy who was selling refurbished printers for $50. I had seen identical printers on eBay for $300, so I bought his entire inventory, put them on eBay for an unbeatable $200, and made $150 on each one. Every week I would go back to the flea market and take the printers off the guy's hands, and every week I was making money. Not much, mind you, but more than I would have been making at McDonald's.

Still, I am not a patient man. I knew nothing happened overnight, but I also knew I had to have a concrete plan. I told myself that I would give myself five years to make my dreams come true and that everything I did from that day forth would be a step in that direction, even if that step seemed a little oblique. I wasn't exactly sure what I hoped to accomplish, but Internet advertising remained at the top of my list. This was a world well worth exploring. Money was flowing from the more traditional venues, such as newspapers and television, to the Internet, and lots of young start-ups were looking for ways to cash in.

DoubleClick was still the Big Kahuna. The company was a leader in brand advertising, luring advertising dollars to the Internet in much the same way newspapers and magazines attracted advertising to their pages. But some of the newer outfits were introducing performance-based advertising. These companies—ValueClick, Advertising.com, Flycast, and others—had software that could track when someone clicked on an ad, and the advertiser was charged only if and when a buyer dragged a mouse across the screen and clicked through. I saw this as a tremendous opportunity. There weren't that many guys in performance-based advertising *yet*, and I thought I could be one of them. What's more, it looked to me as if performance-based advertising was the wave of the future. That model gave advertisers a concrete way of gauging performance, and the company that delivered the most clicks, most consistently, was clearly going to get the most business. DoubleClick might have been the 800-pound gorilla in the world of brand advertising, but its creators could see that the business was changing, and they began to change with it.

In an effort to make sure I understood the intricacies of the business, I started calling around to see what I could learn from anyone who was even remotely connected to Internet advertising. As I mentioned, I was something of an introvert, and I was a little nervous, so I kept practicing my pitch in front of the mirror. I lowered my voice a notch and tried to sound older than my sixteen years. "Hello," I said. "My name is Gary Singh"—Singh is my middle name—"and I do performance-based advertising." That's a fancy word for pay-per-click. "I have a Web site, and I want to know a little about your operation."

I *did* have a Web site, but it was a bit on the cheesy side. Some weeks earlier, thinking ahead, I had used a rudimentary program called Microsoft Frontpage to design it. I'd done a decent job, but it didn't look too professional, and I had promised myself to hire someone to redesign it as soon as I generated a little income. Still, the Web site wasn't critical. I didn't think anyone would actually look at it, and if they did, all they'd learn was that I was an advertising network—like every other fledgling network.

Meanwhile, as a result of these many calls, I was learning something new every day. I discovered, for example, that the vast majority of the Web sites got their ads directly from advertising agencies. A successful ad agency might have ten or twenty clients, but you only needed *one* to get started. If an ad agency took a chance on me, and I delivered, I imagined the doors would swing wide open. And how hard could that be? It was basically a numbers game. He who delivers the big numbers wins.

I kept doing my homework, pumping various companies for information. I needed to know who their customers were; which Web site owners they were working with; how they got paid; and, even more important, how *fast* they got paid. And of course I was very curious about the kind of revenue-sharing agreements that existed among the ad network, the advertiser, and the Web site owners. In other words, who got what piece of the pie?

The Web was virtually limitless, I realized. I just had to convince *one* agency to give me *one* client and I'd be competing with the big boys.

In order to get started, however, I needed to find the right tracking software. I spent a couple of weeks looking around the Internet for a viable program.

Finally, I found a company in London that had a decent tracking system. It was less sophisticated than some of the other stuff I'd seen but looked like it might fit the bill, and I suspected I could get it for a fair price. I picked up the phone and made that first, fateful call. The company turned out to be a one-man operation, and the one man was eager to talk business. A week later, he flew to San Jose to meet me. I hadn't told him I was sixteen, that I was Indian, or that I wore a turban, because I didn't think any of that was germane. I was a businessman, interested in doing business. Period.

We met for dinner at a local Wyndham Hotel. My brother had a driver's license, so he drove me over in Dad's car, and I introduced him as my business partner. I was a little nervous, understandably, because I was eager to strike a deal, but the guy seemed even more nervous than me. He was twenty-one, very pale, and had a pronounced English accent. In the middle of dinner he confessed that he didn't have much money. He said he saw this potential deal as an opportunity to keep his little company from bankruptcy. That certainly helped my cause: He was negotiating from a position of weakness, which immediately put me in the driver's seat. I no longer had reason to be nervous. I had reason to *rejoice*.

By the end of the evening, realizing he had no money for the hotel, I invited him to stay at my parents' house. My brother and I moved into the living room and let him have our room, and in the morning he got up and had breakfast with my family. It was pretty strange. "Who is this white boy?" my mother asked in Punjabi.

"It's fine," I said. "I'm going to make a deal with him. I am trying to do something on the Internet that's even better than those printers I was selling on eBay. Don't worry about it. He won't stay long."

After breakfast, everyone left the house, to go to his or her respective job, but I was on my winter break and I stayed behind with the visitor to talk business. Back in London, he had created a few Web sites, and he was trying to sell ads, though not too successfully. The software was serviceable, but it needed changes, and we talked about how he might rewrite the program. I didn't know anything about programming, mind you; all I knew is what *I wanted the program to do*. So, again, I was thinking like a businessman—thinking about my needs. Still, I knew enough to know that it would never be a great program. In talking to him, it was clear it had its limitations, especially regarding the amount of traffic it could handle—but with some modifications I also knew it would be good enough for my needs. And while I couldn't program it myself, I was certainly able to describe what I needed. At the end of the day, I didn't mind the fact that the program was a long way from state of the art, because that meant I could get it for a reasonable price.

He had dinner with my family the two nights he was there, listening to them speak Punjabi, saying nothing, and on the third day my brother and I took him to the airport. I said I would wait for the changes to the program and sent him on his way.

After he returned to London, we talked on the phone almost every day, and he got busy tinkering with the software. After I took a look at the finished version, I agreed to take the tracking system off his hands for $30,000. I sat down and wrote a simple agreement in which I outlined the general terms and conditions. I am not a lawyer, of course, but I thought I'd done a pretty good job of writing my first contract. And the way I did it was simplicity itself. I went online and did my homework. I looked at dozens of sample contracts, to try to get a handle on the way these things were written, and found everything I needed on the Web. (It's even easier today; you can get a variety of contracts from various sites, at no charge.) The agreement stipulated that I would pay him in ninety days, once I had tested the program, but I already knew that it was working fine. The fact is, I needed those ninety days to generate enough income to pay him—though he didn't need to know that.

I also told him that if things worked out, I might want to hire him to run the software for me, on a month-to-month basis, when the company was up and running, and I men-

tioned the possibility of paying him $10,000 a month. I know
that sounds like a huge number, and it was certainly a huge
number to me, but I had been looking closely at my competition and at the staggering amounts of money that were being
generated, and I knew that all I needed was one little deal to
get my business off the ground.

"Great," he said.

"I'll be in touch," I said.

Suddenly I was in business. I didn't know anything about
computers—not about programming, not about security,
nothing—but I didn't have to. I was a salesman, remember? A
broker. I had the software; all I had to do now was make it
work for me; all I needed were the advertisers and the publishers. If I could get an advertiser to commit to one ad, and if
I could get a Web site owner to put up that ad, there'd be no
stopping me.

The week the deal was signed, I figured out how to incor-
porate online, and I spent $99 to do it. I called my company
Click Agents, and I made myself the marketing director, but I
put the company in my brother's name. I was a minor, and I
didn't want to be breaking the law, and my brother was willing to take the financial risk—which I appreciated. (I certainly
didn't want my parents taking any risks!) Then I began calling
advertising agencies, as I had done during the research-and-
information phase, but this time I was dead serious. I needed

someone to take a chance on me—*anyone*. And it was *hard*. Getting people on the phone was a piece of cake, but finding the person who made the decisions was almost impossible. I would leave one voice-mail, no more—because I didn't want to sound desperate—then follow it up with an e-mail. If I didn't have an e-mail address, I'd guess, which really isn't that complicated. First initial, last name, @whatevercompany.com. And whenever someone actually responded, I was ready. "I have a company called Click Agents," I would say. "We have a consortium of Web sites. I can get your ads on those sites, and I will price them on a per-click basis."

I didn't have a *consortium* of Web sites—I had no real connection to any legitimate Web sites—but they didn't need to know that, and that wasn't the point, anyway. I was a simple salesman. I just had to convince the guy on the other end of the line that I was an effective one. It was the basic theory of supply and demand.

Two days into it, I struck gold. I found myself on the phone with a gentleman at the LeftField Advertising Agency, in San Francisco. LeftField had a client, Infoseek, a search engine, like Google, that was looking to increase traffic to its Web site. "If you put up a $30,000 order, I can deliver traffic at a dollar a click," I told the agency. In plain English, I was telling him that I could deliver at least 30,000 clicks.

"We'll get back to you," I was told.

The following morning, they contacted me with an "insertion order." Suddenly I was in business. That's how fast things moved. In a matter of days, I had a contract for $30,000, which called for me to deliver 30,000 clicks within six weeks. I immediately began to contact every Web site that carried advertising, and I gave them the other part of my pitch: "If you make room for my ads for Infoseek, I will share my revenues with you, fifty-fifty." Most of them accepted—it was a good deal—but there were some that remained unconvinced, and I had to offer them a larger piece of the pie to make it happen. Still, in a matter of days the ads went up, people started clicking, and InfoSeek was getting exactly what it wanted: more traffic. A *lot* more traffic.

Later, as things rolled along, I was able to scale things back to a fifty-fifty split. The Web site owners were making money. I had done my job. Everyone was happy.

"Great delivery, Gary," the guy at LeftField told me. "What do you think you might be able to do for us next month?"

"I can double it."

"Okay. Good. I'll talk to Infoseek and get back to you in a couple of days."

The door was open, and it was up to me to keep it open. I had made a good first impression—which was critical—but I had to keep them impressed.

Did I have a certain skill that made this happen? No, I don't think so. At the end of the day, I was polite, professional, and confident, and that certainly helped. But LeftField had orders to fill—it was in the business of spending money—and I was in the right place at the right time. With the right pitch.

A few days later, that first check arrived. Thirty thousand dollars. I couldn't believe it. I ran to get my brother. "I need you to help me open a bank account," I said.

"Why do you need a bank account?"

"This," I said, showing him the check.

"Wow," he said.

"Yeah," I said. "Wow."

We went to the nearest Bank of America branch and Taj signed for the account, my very first bank account. It was my company, yes, but I was too young to write checks, so I would be relying on Taj to handle the unimaginable sums that were about to begin pouring in.

"Don't tell Dad," I said.

"This isn't illegal, is it?"

"No, of course not. But that's exactly what he'd think."

My brother had total control of the bank account. But who could I trust if not my own brother?

The next day, I hired someone to overhaul my company Web site. I wanted it to look like the portal to a very serious corporation. I needed to impress people. Perception was key.

And the guy did a great job. Anyone looking at the flashy graphics and the 3-D logos must have thought they were dealing with a major player. Most of them probably never even looked at my Web site, of course, which was fine with me. All they knew was that Gary Singh delivered, and that's all they cared about. They had no idea they were dealing with a sixteen-year-old kid because I presented myself as a serious professional. Once again, perception is reality. *That's not a kid on the other end of the line. It's a guy who delivers on his promises.*

Before long, business was booming, and I learned another valuable lesson: People tend to think that in order to start a new business they have to come up with something new and dazzling, but that's a myth—and it's often propagated by venture capitalists. Usually the first question those guys ask you is "What makes you different? Tell me why your company is unlike anything that's out there. If you want our money, you're going to have to show us what makes you so special." What they fail to understand, however—and what most people fail to understand—is that a company can be similar to the competition as long as it has the right people and the right leadership, and as long as it is *committed to being better than all the other players*. In starting Click Agents, I knew I was a small fish in a big pond. After all, I didn't invent performance-based advertising. But as I evolved, I was able to transform my company so that it stood out from the pack—in terms of performance, delivery, professionalism—and that's what got me noticed. My attitude was simple: I knew I could do it, and I knew I could do it better, but I also knew that I wasn't going to be the best coming out of the gate. I would begin by catching up with the other guys, the guys who got there first, and then I'd leave them in the dust. And that's what I did: I overexecuted the competition.

So let me repeat: You don't have to start with a completely new idea. In fact, if you start with something that's *too* different, people might have doubts about your untested model. It might be a brilliant idea, and your model could very well be ahead of its time, but if the investors can't relate to it there's a good chance you're not going to get funded. My advice is to work with something they understand, then turn it into the model you envisioned in the first place. It's a mistake to try to reinvent the wheel when you're coming out of the gate. Start slow and steady, get to parity, then innovate.

Another thing that really helped is that I had a healthy attitude about money. I didn't have to get rich overnight. I was in it for the long haul, and I was looking to build relationships that lasted. The size of the account really didn't matter. What mattered was the way I handled it. If I treated every customer equally, and to the best of my abilities, I knew it would open doors, and that those doors would lead to other, bigger doors. It was one thing to deliver on your promises and another thing to deliver *more* than you promised; I made it a point to try to do the latter. And I generally managed it. At the end of the day, people were looking for results. That's what mattered: results. Results were key. Results inspired confidence, and confidence led to lucrative, long-term relationships.

The lesson here is clear: Never do anything for money— or, at least, *solely* for money. Of course you want to make money, but if that's the only goal, it will adversely affect all of your decisions. They will be colored by greed. So don't let money define the beginning of the journey; make money the rainbow that comes at the end.

This isn't rocket science. If I walk into a store to purchase something, and the clerk is dull and unhelpful, I see a person who has a long, difficult climb ahead of him. But if I get someone who is energetic—who treats me with respect, who takes the job seriously (even if it's a supremely uninspiring job)—I see a person who has the potential to go places. It might not happen that day or that week or that month, but attitude gets you noticed, and the right attitude reaps rewards. It's a simple lesson but an important one. Never relax. Never rest on your laurels. And always look for a way to deliver more than is expected of you. And even when you're doing well, don't get complacent. Stay hungry. And work harder than the competition. In order to stand out in an increasingly crowded field, I had to be better than the rest of them.

Every morning, before I left for school, I would start my day by reviewing a checklist—all the things I needed to do to keep the business running smoothly. Much later, I learned that most businesses do this and that they have a name for that list: key performance indicators (KPIs). This is a simple system they use to measure their progress. It looks at all the variables—customer base, turnover, profitability, debt, and so on—to help determine if there are any weaknesses that need to be addressed. I was doing it by instinct. Then I would look at the daily revenue reports and at the forecasts for the day, the week, the month, and the quarter (hoping I might last an entire quarter!). And when I was done with that, I'd spend a little time looking at what my competitors were up to (new clients, announcements, etc.). Finally, I would roll up my sleeves and begin making calls to potential new advertisers and new publishers.

Before long, I was getting more and more accounts and generating significant amounts of money. I would get a $50,000 order, fill it in record time, and double it the following month. And this was happening over and over again.

But I was still a one-man operation, and that worried me. I had a snazzy Web site, yes, but there were plenty of areas where I felt I was coming up short. I was writing checks by hand, for example, and that looked unprofessional. So I fixed it: I got a simple computer program that generated slick-looking checks. Then there was my answering machine. It was cheap and tinny sounding, so I sprang for my own phone line and a professional voice-mail system. These might seem like minor details, but they are significant: A company that looks good and sounds good inspires confidence. And when a client has confidence in you, he will have no qualms about recommending you to friends and colleagues.

The business continued to grow, but I wanted more. I wanted to get bigger faster, so I did what anyone in my position would do: I began to look around for investors.

Toward that end, I found myself up at a conference in Santa Clara. It had been set up by TiE, an organization established by and for Indian entrepreneurs. (The letters stand for The Indus Entrepreneurs.) I made only one contact in the course of that day, with an Indian gentleman in his mid-forties, but it sounded promising. He agreed to meet with me the following week, at his home in Atherton.

On the appointed day, my brother drove me out to Atherton, undoubtedly one of the wealthiest suburbs in the country. The guy lived in a mansion behind gates. A housekeeper met us at the front door and guided us through the palatial foyer, to the library, where he was waiting for us. I introduced my brother as my business partner, and the man nodded and offered us a drink, which we declined. We then sat across from each other and I began my pitch, telling him a little about Click Agents, which I assured him was on the brink of greatness. He listened without much interest, and I could see his eyes beginning to glaze over. When I paused to take a breath, he started talking about himself and his own accomplishments. The guy was in the semi-conductor business, so I'm not sure he even understood what I was doing, but it didn't really matter: I got the sense that I was there only so he could brag about his phenomenal success.

After the meeting, as my brother and I were driving away, I turned to him and said, "Well, that sure went great."

"It was interesting, anyway," he said.

"I just learned another lesson: Don't expect anyone to help you."

"Well, certainly not that guy. He just wanted to talk about himself."

"At least it wasn't a complete waste of time," I said.

"How's that?"

"If he can do it, I can do it."

Days later, I put that fiasco behind me and decided to keep looking for investors. If people put money into your company, they're saying they believe in you and that they think you're going to succeed, and that's a good thing. So I generated a number of press releases, managed to set up a few meetings, and went off to try to sell myself.

Again, the press releases were not that hard to figure out. I went back to the Internet, that wonderful font of information (and misinformation), and studied a number of press releases. It was a matter of filling in the blanks but doing it creatively. In some ways, it was a shot in the dark, but there are times when that's all it takes. The trick is to give that shot as much direction as possible, and that comes from having information. The more information you have, the more likely you are to hit your target. To paraphrase the Rolling Stones, You're not always going to know exactly what you're doing, but if you try sometimes, and do the legwork, you might get what you need.

Traditionally, these introductory meetings start with the investors telling you a little bit about themselves and about some of their more successful ventures, and when they're done they cede the floor, and it's your turn to wow them. I had no history, of course—I was still a teenager—so I would start by telling them a little about Click Agents and about how well we were doing. Invariably, however, one of these people would interrupt and ask me to back up, to tell them about my prior experience.

"Before Click Agents?" I'd say, wary.

"Yes."

"Well, nothing really. I dropped out."

"Of college."

"No. High school."

"High school?"

"I'm in an accelerated college program now," I said.

At that point, I could see I was losing them—which is probably a good argument for staying in school—and things would generally wind down fairly precipitously. But on at least two occasions there was genuine interest, and it looked as if a deal was a definite possibility. The more I thought about their interest, however, the more it worried me. I was young and inexperienced, and *different looking*, and I suspected that the investors would probably try to replace me. Venture capitalists look for a set persona in a CEO: It's usually a middle-aged, Ivy League–educated, all-American guy, something I was definitely *not*. And while venture capitalists certainly do a lot of good things, there's always the risk that they'll take control. By accepting their investment, you are giving them not only a substantial chunk of the company but the power to make changes. If you're not careful, somebody's golfing buddy might end up taking your job. Remember: They are not investing in your company because they like you or because they are hoping to make the world a better place; they are doing it because they hope to make a lot of money. If you understand that, you might think twice about getting into bed with them. And that's what I did: I decided that—for the time being, anyway—I'd push forward on my own.

So I got back to work, alone, and the business grew, and before long I was making real money. I began to help with the family finances, unusual for a teenager, certainly, but obviously the right thing to do. I'd pick up the tab for the groceries. Or pay for the extra toppings on pizza night. Or spring for a new refrigerator. But I didn't go crazy. I was a first-time businessman. I knew there would be rainy days ahead, and I wanted to be prepared for them. My growing bank account was my insurance policy.

Within six months, I was generating well over $100,000 a month, but it didn't mean that much to me. I knew, instinctively, that there was more to come—much more. I was just getting started. But I wasn't cocky about it. Quite the contrary. There were plenty of people after their own piece of the Internet pie, and if I became complacent—if I let my guard down for even a moment—the results could be disastrous.

That was another lesson: Never lose sight of the competition. I would check their Web sites religiously to see what they were up to. I kept track of any unfamiliar ads. I made lists of companies whose business I was after and figured out how I might approach them.

Throughout this period, my parents were pretty much oblivious to what I was doing. I would work before I left for school, I would check my e-mails and call in for messages while I was at school, and I would work when I got back, but otherwise life went on pretty much as usual. My father would return from the post office at six or seven each evening, and my mother often worked double shifts and didn't get home till eight or nine. I didn't share the details with them—not because I was hiding anything, but because I wanted to retain my independence. Even then, I sensed that it would be important for me to be my own boss, to run my own show.

I didn't share details with my sisters either. Kamal was working as a nurse, and Nirmal was studying to be a nurse, so they were in their own worlds, oblivious.

Taj knew about the money, of course, and he knew that I was selling advertising on the Internet, but he was discreet to a fault, and he also remained focused on his studies, determined to become an engineer. When I needed him to write a check, he wrote it, and he never asked any questions. He never seemed shocked by the amounts either, and he didn't pry.

Finally, unable to take it anymore, I approached my father about dropping out of school, and—after some contained hysterics—he drove me to Accel to have that life-changing conversation with the principal: "My son is going to do bigger things."

The same night, when the family had gathered for dinner, my father looked across the table at me and said. "Okay. Maybe you can tell us exactly what you've been doing all this time."

"You mean with my business?"

"Precisely."

"Are you sure you want to hear this?"

Everyone was staring at me. They all nodded.

"Okay," I said, and I plunged in: "I'm selling advertising, on the Internet, and there are basically three elements at work. First, there's the advertiser. The advertiser has a product or a service and he needs to sell it.

"Next, you have the Web site owners, also known as the publishers—because, just like newspaper publishers, they carry the ads. If I'm reading the news on CNN, for example, and I want to put ads on their site, I have to talk to the people at CNN—or to the people who handle advertising for CNN.

"And last but not least, you have the consumer, regular people who are surfing the net to read articles or get information."

"Go on," my father said.

"What happens is, the consumer goes to the site, takes a look at what he's interested in—a news story, say—and sees an ad on the page. If the ad interests him, he clicks on it and is transported to another Web site.

"If that was one of my ads, one of the ads I had placed on that site, I would get paid by the advertiser for that single click. And of course I'd get paid for every subsequent click. So the more clicks I get, the more money I make—because I'm sending traffic to the advertiser. Pretty simple, huh?"

"But where do you get the ads?" my mother asked.

"From the advertiser," I said. "Or from any agency that handles multiple advertising accounts. That's what I do all day. I call complete strangers and convince them to give me ads."

"And how do you place the ads?" my brother asked.

"I call the Web site owners and convince them to put up the ads. And I give them a little financial incentive to do so."

"It sounds easy," Nirmal said.

"I don't know if it's easy," I said. "But it's a lot more fun than school."

"Maybe you should hire your brother to work for you," my father said.

"I like school," Taj said. He really did. His grade point average never fell below 4.0.

"You'll become an engineer," my father told Taj. "And you'll make fifty or sixty thousand a year. But if you go to work for your little brother, you could become a rich man."

"I'll work for you," Nirmal said. "I don't like school either."

"*You* are staying in school," my father said.

Nirmal looked over at me, frowning. I felt bad for her. I don't want to create the impression that I think school is a bad idea, but it's not for everyone. There are times, certainly, when I wish I spoke fluent French, or Spanish, and I wouldn't mind being able to tell a Cézanne from a Monet, but I'm far more interested in business.

And I'm not interested in business school either, by the way. Everything I know about business I learned as I made my way along, and I'm still learning. I've also learned that the biggest lessons came from my biggest mistakes.

In the days and weeks ahead, freed from school, I felt the adrenaline rush of creating a business from scratch, and I was monomaniacal about it. I wanted to be the best, and I wanted to do it fast. Patience may well be a virtue, but impatience has always worked better for me.

By June, less than three months since I'd dropped out of school, I had achieved revenues approaching $300,000 a month.

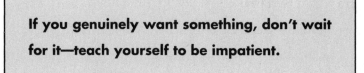

**If you genuinely want something, don't wait for it—teach yourself to be impatient.**

As you might expect from a newly well off kid, I decided it was time to buy my dream car, a Lexus GS400. I took my father and brother with me to the dealership, and there we were, three men in turbans, kicking tires.

I sat inside the car and smelled the new car smell, inhaling it.

"Are there any features this car doesn't have?" I asked.

"No," the salesman replied. "This car is fully loaded."

He was right. There was nothing I could add. It was perfect. I paid for it—$58,000 in cash—and a couple of hours later I drove it off the lot and headed home. My brother was in the seat next to me. My father followed in his Honda. I made a mental note to myself to buy my father a new car when the time was right. I thought he might like a Lexus, too.

By the end of that year, I decided I needed a real office, so one weekend I asked my brother to help me and we went off to look around. I was actually looking for the cheapest, smallest place I could find, because I didn't want to sign the standard five- or seven-year lease. We got lucky and found a tiny space in a very classy building. Ironically, this was the same building where my father had worked as a security guard, right after he arrived in the country, and I asked him to come and have a look at the place too.

"This brings back a lot of memories," he said, "not all of them good."

But he approved of the space. And I took it. And my brother signed the lease on my behalf. It was a little nerve-racking, though. Five thousand a month was a big-ticket item—more than my father's monthly paycheck. I had money in the bank, certainly, but I was always thinking about the worst-case scenario. It's not that I was pessimistic—on the contrary, I genuinely believed in myself—but I was cautious to a fault. I wanted to be ready for that rainy day because I knew that rainy days visited us all.

When I told Taj I wanted him to come work for me, he had his doubts. "How do I know you're going to succeed?" he asked.

"You don't," I said. "But *I* know. And that's all that matters."

I had big dreams. I expected greatness from myself. And, most important, I believed in myself.

The following week, Taj and I raced around town buying furniture. Again I was Mr. McFrugal. I got used, run-of-the-mill stuff from various places, and I went to Office Depot for cheap filing cabinets and equally cheap modular units. My office wasn't being designed to impress anyone. No one would ever come to the office. My business took place on the phone and on the Internet. The office was strictly for me and for the staff I would try to put together in the months ahead. I had 1,200 square feet of space, enough room for half a

*Gurbaksh with siblings (from left) Taj, Nirmal, and Kamal at Click Agents' first office (1999).*

dozen people, and I was looking for salespeople. At that point, more than anything else, I needed more commitments from the ad agencies and from the Web site owners. It was all about volume.

When we settled into the new office, I realized that in my correspondence with my clients I could create the illusion of power. My return address didn't mention Suite 312; instead, it directed all correspondence to the *Third Floor.* I wanted them to think I had 50,000 square feet of space, with commanding city views in every direction. That is the stereotype of a successful business, and the lesson here is basically this: Stereotypes make people comfortable. I decided to try to come across as the stereotypical businessman, no matter what it took. And stereotypes can be defined both by the way you look and by the way you present yourself and your company. It's all about making the other guy comfortable. Once you get to that stage, you're in a position to actually do business.

I don't know if my brother was impressed by what I was doing, but he was sufficiently impressed to leave college without his bachelor's degree. He came to work for me as head of Human Resources.

Since we couldn't afford to hire experienced personnel, we put ads on monster.com and in the *San Jose Mercury-News*, and before long Taj was lining up interviews with prospective employees. We were looking for anyone who was hungry and motivated, and we were willing to take risks on promising, untested candidates. The most important thing for me was to decide if a person was the right fit, and both Taj and I turned out to be pretty good judges of character. Before long, we had a dozen employees squeezed into that tiny space, and all of them worked out. Their lack of experience also helped, since we were able to train them to do things exactly the way we wanted them done.

I also hired my sister Kamal. She was working as a nurse, and though she found the work rewarding, she was interested in exploring new things.

"What would I do?" she asked.

"Your job will be to manage relationships with the publishers—the Web site owners. They need to know that the ads are up. If we have a contract for a given number of ads, it'll be your job to see that we deliver on those numbers."

"How much are you paying?" she asked, smiling.

"Not much," I said. "But there will be dividends down the road."

As we got down to the business of business, it became immediately clear that I was the boss. I was strict, and I expected results, and I believe the employees respected that. I was approachable as a boss, certainly, but not terribly approachable as a person, because I focused solely on the business. If some guy thought he could come into my office to tell me he'd just been dumped by his girlfriend, he thought wrong. I wasn't heartless, but I didn't care about the girlfriend. Everyone was there to work. They were getting paid for it, and I expected them to leave their personal lives at home. I didn't whine to them about not having a girlfriend, or about never having had a girlfriend, or about the fact that I didn't even know how to go about *getting* a girlfriend, and I was pretty sure they weren't interested. The lack of interest didn't make them bad people; it made them good workers. And that's what I wanted to focus on: work. This was my first venture as a businessman, and I was determined to succeed. My goal was to turn us into an army, and an army won't function well if people lose sight of the goal. The goal is simple: winning (in both business and war). My job was to keep the soldiers focused on that goal, but that didn't mean I had to be heartless and uninvolved. Despite my desire to keep personal issues out of the office, some of my colleagues became like family to me. Throughout this period I learned that—at the end of the day—it's about finding the right balance between humanity and relentlessness in reaching your bottom-line goals.

With two of my employees, however, there was a brief period of adjustment: My brother, Taj, and my sister, Kamal. I had gone from being the little brother to being the boss, and it must have been odd for them to see me running the show. But when they realized that I knew what I was doing, and that I was committed to the company, they never questioned me.

I practically lived in the office. I'd get there early, grab a fast-food lunch, and work well into the night, and half the time I crashed on my fake-leather couch. I was not in the best shape of my life, and I had absolutely no social life (which wasn't such a big deal, since I'd never had a social life). All I really wanted was to succeed, and while I was more reasonable when it came to others, I sacrificed everything to make it happen: health, family, balance, and—most of all— my youth.

On the rare occasions when I made it home for a meal, I always heard the same refrain: *You don't look well. You need to take a break from time to time. It's not healthy to think only about work.* Yet my family understood that sacrifices were necessary, that everything we had, modest as it was, was a result of their hard work, so they weren't about to stop me from pursuing my own dream.

I remember coming home for dinner the day I closed a deal with Providian Bank, which at $200,000 was the single biggest deal in the company's brief history. We had a month to fulfill our obligations, which meant that we'd be turning $100,000 profit on that account alone. My father said, "It would take your mom and me three years of work to make that money."

"And that's only one account," Taj said.

It seemed unreal to them, and in many ways it was beyond their understanding, but I loved this brave new world of Internet advertising, and I felt very much at home in it.

Then reality reared its ugly head. The guy who had sold me his software for $30,000, and who was being paid $10,000 a month to keep the technology running, called from London to tell me that he wasn't happy with the deal we'd made.

This is my recollection of how the conversation went:

"I believe I'm entitled to one-third of the company," he said.

"This company is successful because I made it success-ful," I said. "And I'm using your software, yes, but I own it."

"That's not the way I see it," he said.

"Then please explain it to me," I said. "When we met, you were on the verge of bankruptcy, so I don't know what you're complaining about. The fact that this company is more successful than you ever thought it would be doesn't mean you're entitled to a penny more than the $30,000 we agreed to. We had a deal, and we both signed it."

"I don't give a damn about that deal," he replied. "You owe me."

"I don't owe you anything. If you want to come to work for me, full time, I'll bump your salary and we can talk about the future. But I created this company."

"I don't want a bleeding salary. I want a third of the company."

"That's not going to happen," I said.

"If you're going to be greedy about it, I'll shut you down."

"You're threatening me?"

"You just watch."

The next day, as threatened, he shut me down. The servers were located at a company called Frontier Global Center, located in Santa Clara, not far from San Jose, and the account was still in his name. So all he had to do was make a call and take the servers off-line. It was devastating. He shut me down and I was powerless to do anything about it. When I contacted the people at Frontier Global, they were polite and apologetic, but they couldn't help because he controlled the account. Worse still, he owed them money, and Frontier Global had been after him about that for several months.

I went so far as to call the San Jose branch of the Federal Bureau of Investigation, but they weren't any help either. This wasn't the type of case they handled, they told me. My father called and reached another officer, and he was told the same thing. The FBI only handled much bigger cases, and it was already backlogged, so the chances of getting around to my case were slim to none. "So my son is paying taxes, but the government can't help him because he's one of the little guys?" my father asked.

"If that's the way you want to look at it, I can't do anything about it," the officer replied. "I am just describing the reality of the situation."

We considered filing a police complaint, but computer crimes weren't within their jurisdiction, and we couldn't find the guy anywhere because he'd moved out of his apartment and had left no forwarding address. For all I knew, he might have been living in San Jose.

At that point I realized that this was the rainy day I'd been expecting. I again called Frontier Global, the company that ran the servers, and asked how much he owed them. It turned out to be in excess of $100,000, and they had considered shutting him down, but if they had done that they would have never seen their money. The Mafia has a similar approach: Don't kill a guy who owes you or you'll never collect.

"I can pay off that debt," I said. "But I want to take over the account."

"Fine," they said.

Then I told my brother to find someone with enough technical expertise to run the software for us. "I need him now!" I wailed. "Today!"

We were off-line for an entire week. Can you imagine a week without e-mail? A week without the Web? Well, that was the lifeblood of my business, and that week almost put me under. The ads weren't appearing on the Web sites, and the advertisers weren't getting any traffic. They couldn't even log on to view their own accounts! It was a complete disaster. Time on the Internet is measured in dog years. For that entire week, Click Agents had ceased to exist.

All week I refused to answer my phone. I didn't know what to say. What was I supposed to tell my customers: We'll be back next week?

That wasn't going to do anything for them, especially if I wasn't up and running. My goal was to get back online, and that was my *only* goal.

On the seventh day, we were back, and that's when I began trying to make amends. It had been a hellacious week, and I had avoided absolutely everyone, even at the risk of pissing them off, because I knew that nothing I could have said or done would have made them happy. I could have told them "My programmer screwed me," which was the truth, but it wasn't exactly confidence inspiring. What kind of fool was I, that I had let a greedy programmer bring me to my knees? The experience taught me another valuable lesson: Never put yourself in a position of vulnerability.

And that wasn't the only lesson I learned. I also learned that damage control can happen only once you've got the situation in hand. At that point I could get on the phone to my clients and make my apologies: "Sorry. We had serious technological issues. I know it's unacceptable, but you have my word that it won't happen again. Please let me know how I can make it up to you."

I gave them credit, I gave them free advertising, and—for a period—I even gave the publishers a slightly larger percentage than they'd contracted for. And you know what? It worked.

I didn't lose a single customer. The following month we did $200,000 in business and we began to work our way back toward record levels. In the meantime, I took steps to make sure nothing like that disaster ever happened again. I spoke to Frontier Global, who recommended a technological whiz kid, and I had him make sure our program was secure. Often a programmer leaves a "back door" open that allows him to sneak inside and fiddle with the software; this new whiz kid found three such portals and quickly shut them down. I was back in control, and I intended to be in *total* control. To that end, I hired a chief technology officer (CTO) and several engineers and put them on the Click Agents' payroll—at generous salaries. I was trying to *unlearn* some of the lessons I'd picked up from the many years of shopping at McFrugal's. Everyone likes a good deal, but you can't cut corners where it counts.

That experience taught me three valuable lessons. The first was to expect the unexpected. Life is full of surprises, not all of them pleasant, so it's wise to be prepared. Think about your choices, about the people you're dealing with, and about the consequences of even the smallest decisions.

The second lesson was equally valuable: Own your mistakes. I'd been in business with a rogue who almost destroyed me, but I'd made the decision to work with him, so the mistake was mine. Click Agents was my company. I was responsible for it. When I was scrambling to control the damage, I never once suggested I was blameless. I took responsibility for the mistake, and it worked.

And the final lesson is the one I just mentioned: Be frugal, but don't be cheap. Some corners aren't meant to be cut, especially when it comes to hiring the right personnel.

The rogue disappeared, defeated, and immediately there-after I started making big changes. For starters, I hired a law firm to draw up the contracts with my CTO and the two en-gineers. I didn't intend to repeat the mistake I'd made with the original programmer, when I thought I understood con-tracts. In addition, I talked to those same lawyers about some kind of stock option plan for my employees. This wasn't sim-ple generosity; it was good business sense: I wanted a piece of something really big rather than 100 percent of something re-ally small. Click Agents was growing, and it was going to keep growing—it wasn't your basic corner liquor store, where sales don't really change much from one year to the next—and I wanted to make sure that everybody's interests were aligned. To that end, I was willing to give away some of the company. The goal was to make sure everyone was invested—to create an environment where people cared.

From that point on, whenever I hired someone, stock op-tions were part of the package, which made the job that much more attractive. As to those employees who were already there, the best of them were grandfathered into the deal.

**The lesson here is simple. Be generous; it works.**

I got back to business and worked hard to make up for lost time. Within a year, I had twenty employees—salesmen, programmers, marketing people—and was generating north of $1 million a month. It was a real company, and I had become a real CEO, making a very modest $60,000 a year. I never gave myself a raise, though. I didn't need it. I couldn't have spent that $60,000 anyway, and by not giving myself a raise I was fattening the company's coffers—and a large part of those coffers belonged to me.

There were times when I didn't really believe all these good things were really happening. I kept taking the company to the next level, and to the next level after that, but sometimes I'd look at my reflection in the mirror—at that turbaned seventeen-year-old, staring back at me—and I'd be filled with doubt. Up until that point, I'd been operating almost exclusively on the phone, doing business with people who had no idea I was just a kid. But the company was evolving at a spectacular rate, and I knew that someday soon I would have to come out of hiding. I began to give serious thought to getting rid of the turban.

Still, it was a very tough decision. In the Sikh religion, males are required to wear turbans, and they are not permitted to cut their hair—*ever*. The turban didn't mean that much to me—with or without it, I was still a Sikh—but over the years I had been ridiculed for wearing it, and this had caused me more than my fair share of anguish. I wanted to talk to my father about the possibility of removing it and of cutting my hair, but I knew he would never agree to it, and I was deeply conflicted.

For a time, I tried not to think about this. I put it out of my mind and focused on growing my business. Click Agents was becoming a force in the advertising world. We were noticed for all the right reasons: We were reliable, we produced results, and we were beginning to separate from the pack.

Whenever I walked into the office, I would think, *Here I am, where I belong.* I loved work. I loved success. I would reach my desk, take a seat, and it was almost like a hit of adrenaline. *How do I make today an even better day than yesterday?* I would ask myself. *What do I have to do to leave the competition in the dust?*

Seriously, now—who could ask for anything more?

The First
$40 Million 3

**A**s 1999 got under way, Silicon Valley was still caught up in the dot-com euphoria. Wall Street was as strong as ever, and the Nasdaq was going through the roof. Venture capitalists were still spending obscene amounts of money on start-ups whose entire value was their tenuous connection to the Internet; college kids with vague ideas became instant millionaires; and companies with unproven business models were still executing IPOs, their crazy stock prices based on little more than the relative novelty of the dot-com concept. Everyone wanted to *get big fast*, and there was so much venture capital around that just about all of them were given a chance to do so. Lots of these new companies *did* get rich, but the vast majority went bust. Most of them you never heard of; some might ring a faint bell: Pets.com. Flooz.com. Kozmo.com. Etoys.com. Webvan.com. Boo.com (one of the biggest disasters in dot-com history). The list of casualties was endless.

There was one thing that set Click Agents apart from the many failures, however, and it was pretty simple: We were actually making money. We were a viable business. We had nothing to prove.

In January 2000, less than a year after my official launch, I got a call from an investment banker in New York. "I hear Click Agents is doing very well," he said. "Have you thought about selling your company?"

He flew out from New York to meet me, and I was actually a little nervous. I was seventeen years old, and I had a beard, which made me look a little older, but I also had a turban, and I was frankly worried about the kind of impression I was going to make. He didn't seem at all put out—or, if he was, he didn't show it. "I'm going to put together a list of companies that might be interested in buying you, and we'll go through the list together, and then we'll pitch Click Agents to them for a hundred million dollars."

I don't mean to be immodest here, but that didn't seem like an unreasonable number. Other companies that had no business being in business, and were in fact slated for the slag heap of dot-com history, had been evaluated at much higher prices, so this was actually a reasonable number. I was being valued on performance, results, and revenue, unlike some of those other companies, which were still talking about their *potential*. My fundamentals were real. I was running an actual business.

A few weeks later, the investment banker arranged for me to fly to New York to meet with the brass at DoubleClick, the company that had initially sparked my interest in this whole crazy business. I was a little nervous, understandably, but on my way to the meeting I kept telling myself to be fearless. That's key in any business situation. If you show fear, they sense weakness, and that can be deadly. You must always negotiate from a position of strength. *They want me*, I kept telling myself. *They need me.*

When I arrived, I was in total awe of their offices. They had sleek, high-end furnishings, magnificent views of the Hudson River, and a basketball court on the roof. It was an incredibly posh environment, the exact opposite of our offices in

San Jose, and this only added to my tension. Still, the meeting went very well. None of them seemed fazed by either my youth or my appearance, and they listened attentively when it was my turn to speak. I described my performance-based model, talked about the speed at which the company was growing and about our profitability, and when I left their swank offices I felt as if I had definitely piqued their interest.

By the time I got back to San Jose, though, it was clear that DoubleClick was not going to be buying Click Agents, but they did arrange for us to meet with ValueClick, another big player. I flew down to Los Angeles and took a cab to the ValueClick offices in West Lake Village—I was too young to rent a car—where I met with Jim Zarley, the CEO, and a couple of other executives, including Sam Paisley. The conversation was a little awkward, mostly because I needed to protect my company's ideas, and I was careful not to reveal too much about our business model. Still, I knew what they wanted to hear, and I wasn't shy about discussing the bottom line: Click Agents was a hugely profitable company, and it was continuing to grow at a robust pace.

But I didn't have to say much beyond that. In the middle of our guarded conversation, I got the distinct impression that they had already made up their minds. They needed us—we were taking away market share—and they were eventually going to buy us. Maybe not that day, or the day after that, or even in the next month or two, but I was confident it would happen before long.

> **The experience taught me another lesson: Don't tell people what they ask you, tell them what they need to hear to fall in love with you.**

On my way out of the office, I overheard a few whispered comments about the turban, and I found it more than a little disturbing. These people were either bigoted or plain stupid. The turban is a religious symbol, no different from a gold crucifix or a yarmulke, and I thought the behavior of those few employees was both childish and disrespectful.

On the flight home, I couldn't stop thinking about it, and I was still thinking about it long after I'd landed. Up until that point, I had been a disembodied voice, communicating on the phone or via e-mail, hidden away in my office. But my company was evolving, and it was time to show my face to the world. I needed to be comfortable with my appearance.

Two weeks later, I found out that DoubleClick had decided to invest in ValueClick, not in Click Agents, which was not totally unexpected. In March, with the Nasdaq at over

5000 and close to peaking, ValueClick came out with an initial public offering (IPO). It sold for $18 a share, becoming one of the last companies to go public before the dot-com bust. The price quickly shot up to $24, but it began to sink almost immediately, and it dropped all the way to $7. At that point, I knew it wouldn't be long before I heard from ValueClick again. The company would be looking for an investment to boost its value, and we were just the ticket. Click Agents was still going strong and still making serious money.

As I waited for that to happen, I remembered that first meeting with ValueClick, and I went to see my sister, Kamal. She was in her office, working away.

"I need you to do me a favor," I said.

"What?"

"Go with me to get my hair cut."

"What? Are you crazy? Dad is going to kill you!"

"I don't care," I said.

We got into my Lexus and drove to Supercuts. When we walked inside, everyone turned to stare. *A guy with a turban getting a haircut. How weird is that?* Suddenly I was afraid to my very core. Maybe my father would never forgive me.

I could feel my heart beating like crazy.

"You all right?" my sister asked.

"No," I said. "But my mind's made up."

When it was my turn, I sat in the chair, removed my turban, and let seventeen years' worth of hair fall to my shoulders. "Cut it," I said.

"All of it?"

"Well, no. Just, you know—I want a regular haircut, like a regular person."

In less than an hour, it was gone. I looked in the mirror and hardly recognized myself, but I liked what I saw.

Kamal and I got back into the Lexus and made our way back to the office. "You look so different," Kamal said.

I took my eyes off the road and found her staring at me. "Different good or different bad?" I asked.

"Neither. Just different. It's going to take me a while to get used to it."

"I like it," I said. "Maybe people will actually stop staring when I walk into a room."

"Maybe," she said, "but you better brace yourself for Mom and Dad."

"I don't know why they're going to be upset," I said. "I'm still me. I love my family, I love my culture, and I love my religion. The only thing that has changed is my physical appearance, and I don't need to be defined through the way I look."

"Well, if I were you, I'd still brace myself," she said.

When I walked into the office, I got a lot of strange looks from the employees, but they said nothing, and they got used to it pretty quickly. What choice did they have? I was the boss.

Out in the street, the change was instant. Without the turban, people no longer noticed me, and I loved it. I could walk into Starbucks, stop for a magazine, pump gas, and I was *just like everybody else*. It felt great.

Deep down inside, though, I was still the same guy. I was still a proud Sikh through and through. In removing the turban, I wasn't less of a Sikh and I wasn't disavowing my religion. And in fact I didn't believe that in cutting my hair I would be somehow offending God. With or without the turban, I was a man of faith. I knew that without faith nothing was possible and that with faith nothing was impossible.

At the end of the day, issues of faith notwithstanding, I still had to face my parents, and when I walked through the front door of the house my heart started again beating like crazy. My mother was the first to see me, and her mouth dropped open in shock. She was so horrified that she couldn't speak. She turned away and walked out of the room, supporting herself against the walls. "Just wait until your father gets home," she said weakly.

I waited, growing increasingly nervous. Months earlier, when the idea of getting rid of the turban first began to percolate, I had thought about asking for his blessing, but I knew that it was never going to happen. And if I had gone ahead and done it at that point, against his stated wishes, it would have been much worse. Still, this was bad enough, and I was bracing myself for a real firestorm when he came home.

The moment he walked through the front door, he delivered on my expectations. "I cannot believe you did this!" he said, shouting. "You disrespect your family, and, worse, you disrespect your religion."

"It has nothing to do with respect or with religion," I said.

"I came to this country to make a new life, but I never lost my faith!" he continued, drowning me out. "You are a coward! You are a huge disappointment to me! I will remember this day as one of the most disappointing days of my life!"

It was all I could do not to burst into tears, but the Chahal men seldom express emotion. It hurt, though, to have disappointed my father. As every child knows, letting your parents down can be painful. At the end of the day, though, even in that tough, emotional state, I knew I had made the right decision. Life is about choices, and you can't make everyone happy, so at some point you have to learn to live for yourself. This applies in business situations too, by the way. When you make decisions, it's fine to listen to the people around you, but the final decisions need to be yours. If you can't trust yourself to make decisions, you'll never succeed. And if you make the wrong decision from time to time, don't sweat it—you won't make the same mistake again.

For weeks and months afterward, I would look up to find my parents staring at me as if I were a stranger. And in some ways I *was* a stranger. My father had come to America to live out his dream, only to find that his son had dreams of his own.

For a period, I avoided my parents and they avoided me. I found myself spending more time with my grandmother, who was in declining health. She was in the early stages of Alzheimer's, and there were days when it was impossible for her to connect the dots. Sometimes she didn't know who I was. I would sit with her, holding her hands in mine, and patiently answer her questions.

"What are you doing for work?" she would ask again.

"I have a company that makes a lot of money, and I think I'm going to be selling it for millions of dollars," I said. "We're going to be rich. Good things are in store for the whole family. What do you think of that? Your grandson is a big success."

"Success? Success is to be married with three children. *That* is success."

I'm sure she believed that, but it would have been nice if she'd been clear-headed enough to be happy for me. Half the time she confused me with my brother, who was not married either. And she was fixated on this marriage business. Two or three times a week she'd ask me why I wasn't married, and wondered what I was waiting for. "You are not a young man anymore," she would say.

"I'm seventeen," I protested, laughing.

"Seventeen is not young," she replied.

In late summer, shortly after I turned eighteen—and several months after ValueClick went public—I got the call I'd been expecting. "We want to take our discussions to the next level," Jim Zarley said.

I called a meeting to discuss this with key people on my staff, many of whom were heavily vested in the company. I had received a merger call, I told them, and it sounded serious, so I needed to make sure that everything was running smoothly. "If we are going to do this, we need to make sure all our ducks are in order. Are we collecting on time? Are we exceeding our sales forecast? Are we getting the best rates from our publishers? I need you guys to make sure everything is running perfectly, because for the next few weeks I'm going to be focused on the deal, and I won't be around to look over your shoulders. Nothing has changed, okay? I need you guys to keep doing your jobs, only I need you to do them better than ever."

On November 1, 2000, ValueClick agreed to buy Click Agents in a $40 million all-stock merger. We would be getting 5.3 million shares based on a $7.50 per share price. As part of the deal, we would all go to work for ValueClick, and I would sign a three-year noncompete agreement. This agreement meant I couldn't do anything remotely connected to Web advertising for another three years, until I was twenty-one, but that didn't bother me at all. I was about to become a very rich eighteen-year-old.

To the casual observer, it might have seemed that success came too easily and too quickly, but I don't think that's the case. The sale of Click Agents had nothing to do with mindless Internet euphoria. It was bought based on real metrics. I was profitable. I was making money. I was growing. So it wasn't about luck or timing, it was about having real assets—assets somebody wanted. And that didn't happen by accident. I did what I thought I had to do to succeed: I tried to build a great company that was in it for the long term, and I did it by making sure the foundations were solid. If you have an idea for a company, that's just the beginning—that's your entry point. What really matters is execution. Don't think about the millions you're going to make; think instead about creating a company that will be *worth* millions. It sounds like I'm splitting hairs, but I'm not: The difference is huge. Success is largely about *substance*. If your company is about real, tangible assets, and you're looking at the long term (not the quick hit), you are going be handsomely rewarded for it.

> **Don't chase the money. Chase substance. If you have substance, the money will follow.**

The day after the deal closed, I celebrated with my family. We went to the local *gurdwara* and thanked God for this great blessing. A Sikh priest led the prayers, and he noted that my father's dreams of a new life in America had indeed come true. "Perhaps not in the way he envisioned them, but they have come to pass nonetheless," he said.

Then we went back to the house and had dinner, overwhelmed by our good fortune, but it wasn't until I woke up the next morning that it actually hit me: I was a millionaire many times over.

Of course, I was only a millionaire on paper. It's not as if the cash was sitting in the bank, waiting for me. In fact, I had to protect it. I had to report for work that morning and in mornings to come with one goal and one goal only: to increase the value of my stock—not only for myself, but for every shareholder in the company.

In December, a month after the deal closed, we moved into new offices in Fremont. A couple of months earlier, just before our one-year lease had come up for renewal, the landlord informed us that there were dozens of dot-com

*The Click Agents team at the company Christmas party in 2000 (Gurbaksh in front).*

companies looking for office space and that he intended to triple our rent. I thought this was outrageous, and I didn't think I needed to be in the heart of San Jose, so my brother and I looked elsewhere and found that space in Fremont. The price was right, and there was a bonus. Parts of the city were predominantly Indian, so we knew we'd always eat well.

Every eight or nine days, however, I had to fly south to Los Angeles, for one meeting or another at the ValueClick offices. The first time I flew in, as you may recall, I had to take a cab to the office, because I was too young to rent a car. At that point, not wanting my new partners to freak out over my youth, I did what I had to do: I went on craigslist.com and got a fake ID. It was cheap and simple, and nobody got hurt—not the car rental agencies, not the L.A. drivers, and not me. I know I broke the law, a *little*, and I'm not proud of it, but I believe the statute of limitations on this particular crime has long since expired.

The partnership with ValueClick didn't go as smoothly as I had hoped. In very short order, I found myself stifled by the corporate environment. There were endless meetings, but nothing ever seemed to get accomplished, and half the time I didn't even know what we were meeting about. And neither did the corporate executives, apparently. The company was losing value every day. By the time my deal officially closed, the share price had dropped to $4, so my stake had plummeted by almost $20 million. It was crazy. I had been given 5.3 million shares at $7.50 a share, and my principal interest—my *job*, really—was to push the share price to stratospheric levels. But I was feeling as if I couldn't get anyone to listen to my ideas, and they seemed unmotivated in the extreme.

I'll give you one telling example: The company had $200 million in the bank, money it could have been investing in manpower, products, and technology—but everyone was so risk-averse that they refused to touch it. When you have $200 million in cash available, in my opinion, you should be doing something with it, not simply enjoying the interest you're collecting. The interest on that chunk of change paid for ValueClick's operations, and then some, of course, but it wasn't growing the company. Instead, the company was stagnating. Sitting on your money is not a strategy; it's an *absence* of strategy.

I wasn't the only one affected by the drop in price, of course. Every shareholder was affected, though some meant more to me than others: Two and a half million of those 5.3 million shares belonged to some of the people who worked with me at Click Agents, including my brother and sister. The company had been set up as a meritocracy, and the employees who had helped turn Click Agents into a success were rewarded for their contributions. At the end of the day, though, I was the one who had made the decision to sell the company, and I felt a huge responsibility. Even so, despite my continued efforts, ValueClick wasn't giving me a chance to stop the downward slide. It seemed the people there weren't listening to or interested in investing in my ideas. This was incredibly frustrating to me because we were at polar extremes on a very important issue: Their attitude was: *Don't fix it if it's not broken.* Mine has always been: *Fix it before it breaks.* And I can tell you from experience that my strategy works much better over the long term.

To be brutally honest, I got the impression that most of the people in the company were focusing their energies on impressing the two head guys, Jim and Sam. There was a lot of ass-kissing going on, which is not something I have ever been able to relate to. Running a company isn't about making each other feel good. It's about business. Anything that doesn't pertain directly to the business is counterproductive. There's really no room for it in the office environment. As a boss, ass-kissing is not high on my list of needs. All I ask of my employees is that they do their jobs, that they do them well, and that once they are doing them well they make an effort to do them better. I'm a guy who cares about three things: results, results, and results. But some of the people at ValueClick seemed to be mostly concerned about brownie points.

Every time the share price dropped a little, it hurt me more than it hurt Jim and Sam. I had more shares than both those guys *combined*. In short order, it became pretty obvious to me that Jim and Sam resented me for my stake in the company, and I didn't understand why. If I'd been given 5.3 million shares, it was obviously because Click Agents had been worth it. But they didn't see it that way. I wasn't even half their age. I had more money. They couldn't get their heads around that. They appeared to be jealous. And you know, there was a lesson in this, too. (I'm a firm believer that you can learn from other people's mistakes.) Learn to deal with jealousy. As you make your way up the ladder, people are going to wonder *Why him? Why not me?* Don't sweat it.

There's no getting away from that. And of course there's a flip side to the lesson: Don't *be* jealous. Jealousy is one of the most useless emotions on the planet.

My salary had also jumped, from $60,000 to $150,000, but this didn't mean much to me. When you have a stake in a company, the paycheck is the least of it. It's really about growing the company. I would have gladly taken a *cut* if I felt I was working with a strong, dynamic team that was focused on our collective future.

During those first few months, ValueClick made several other acquisitions, including the purchase of ZMedia, a company at the forefront of e-mail marketing. ZMedia's offices were in the San Jose area, so they ended up moving into our space in Fremont. One of the people who came over was Troy Baloca, a loud, colorful character who also happened to be a smart businessman. We hit it off right away, and we began to hang out together. From time to time we'd go out for a drink and whine about the guys at the head office. (We did this outside the office, never in the office. In the office it was always 100 percent business.) They seemed locked in an us-versus-them mentality, I noted. They were ValueClick, we were Click Agents, and we had next to nothing in common. At best, we were the stepchildren, and we were to be accepted as part of the "package," but we would never be part of the family. I continued to share ideas and make suggestions, but everything I said fell on deaf ears. At one point, I found out that we were going after the same accounts. I had just closed a huge deal with a major advertiser, and two days later I was undercut by one of the people at the head office.

"It's insane," I told Troy. "We're supposed to be on the same team."

Troy didn't disagree with me, but he tried to take my mind off the unpleasantness by forcing me to live a little. We went to dinner from time to time and to some of the local clubs, and I started getting very interested in girls, but I was still too terrified to approach them.

"I don't know what you're afraid of," Troy kept telling me. "I've got a great woman at home, and I love her, and any day now I'm going to pop the question. That's what it's all about."

I was happy for Troy, but he was about ten years older than me, and I figured I had time to catch up. Oddly enough, despite the friendship, I hadn't told him that I was eighteen. I guess I still thought it would affect my credibility. Meanwhile, I tried to focus on getting a little credibility with the ladies. "As soon as I see a woman I like, I'll make my move," I said. That was just talk, of course. I didn't even know what a *move* was.

Still, Troy was showing me that there was life outside business. I tried foods I'd never tried before, and I even had a drink from time to time. And on more than one occasion, fortified by Grey Goose vodka, I even ventured onto a dance floor. I also started paying a little more attention to the clothes I wore, though clearly I was still a victim of McFrugal's: My very favorite store was Ross Dress for Less.

Meanwhile, I went into the office every day, Monday to Friday, and tried to do my job. I was working for a multibillion-dollar, Nasdaq-listed company, and I was the youngest executive ever to hold such a position. I suppose I should have been proud and happy. But no; I was miserable.

To compound matters, my original programmer—the guy from London, the guy who shut me down for that whole, hellacious week—decided to sue me. He had read about the deal with ValueClick—big news at the time, hard to miss—and came after me with guns blazing. I was subjected to an endless round of depositions, in front of a video camera, and subjected to questions that were impossible to answer. If you said yes, you were wrong; if you said no, you were equally wrong. This is standard operating procedure. Attorneys will tell you that depositions are designed to hurt you. The common tactic is to use *argumentative* questions, and the classic question—after a couple of easy ones ("Is your name Gurbaksh Chahal?" "Do you live in San Jose?")—is: "Have you stopped beating your wife?" There's no way to answer that without losing. No matter what you say, you're guilty. And anything that pushed my buttons strengthened their case. They had so-called body language experts standing by, ready to review the videotapes, and if I expressed any discomfort whatsoever, it would be easy for them to report that I was lying. It was all I could do to keep myself from falling apart, and every hour or so I would excuse myself to go to the men's room, where I would splash cold water on my face and try to talk myself down. "You will not get angry! You will not lose it! You will answer their questions honestly and calmly, and you will get through this."

It was psychological warfare, and I survived, but only because I knew I had done nothing wrong. We had a contract. It was written by a sixteen-year-old, admittedly, but it was still a contract, and we had both walked into the deal with our eyes open.

Still, at the end of the day, my lawyer urged me to settle. "This isn't about right and wrong," he said. "Litigation seldom is. It's about greed. He saw that big number—forty million bucks—and he wants a piece of it."

"He got everything I promised him and more," I said. "And that big number isn't so big anymore."

"Gurbaksh, you're not listening to me. That's not the point. It will cost you too much to litigate this thing. I'm urging you to settle."

At the end of the day, I realized he was right. I wrote a big check and made the guy go away.

> **The experience taught me another lesson: Pick your battles.**
>
> **I learned something else, too. We live in the most litigious society on the planet, so I have three little words of advice: *Watch your back.***

Some weeks later, perhaps feeling that I'd been catapulted into adulthood by that harrowing ordeal, I decided it was time to leave home. I wanted to show my parents that I was independent. As long as I lived at home, my father's word was law, and I wanted to get away from that—I wanted to control my own life, my own future.

I remember the night I told my parents. I had just returned from work, resigned to getting it over with, and walked into the house to find them arguing. The issue seemed minor, and I was eager to get my problem off my chest, so I simply interrupted them. "Mom, Dad, I've decided to move out," I said. They ignored me and kept arguing, their voices growing louder and more strident. So I repeated it: "Did you hear me? I'm moving out! I'm leaving home!"

They both turned to face me, still angry, and they both said the same thing at the exact same moment: "Good!"

It was kind of funny, actually.

Later, when they'd resolved their differences, we talked about my imminent departure like adults, and they had a hard time wrapping their minds around it. "Why would you want to leave this house, where everything is provided for you?" my father said. And my mother concurred: "How will you manage? You are a still a boy. You don't even know how to boil water."

I understood their concerns. I had led a pretty sheltered life, and it wasn't going to be easy, but it's what I wanted. And when I wanted something, I always made it happen. Not even their tears could keep me from leaving home.

When it became increasingly apparent that I wasn't about to change my mind, my parents began to panic a little. They continued to try to talk me out of it. "Why would you leave your family? Indian families do not do this. It is tradition to live together." They were right, in fact. In a typical Indian household, sons *never* leave their parents; they stay with them even after they marry. But I was leaving at eighteen, as a single man, and they found it incomprehensible. "What are you not getting from us? Don't you like it here?"

"No. I like it here fine. I just want to try something new."

For an American family, this is no big deal. But my family had come to this country with a very specific vision of the future, and in those dreams we would always be a big, happy family, *living together under the one roof.*

"This is what we worked for?" my father asked. "For our son to leave the house? For our youngest son to abandon us?"

And from my mother: "Look how old we've become! Who's going to take care of us now?"

The guilt gnawed away at me, but I still went out and began looking around for apartments—sometimes with my brother, sometimes with my friend Troy.

Eventually I found a very nice place in Fremont, a few blocks from the Indian section of the city and only about ten minutes from our offices. It was a new building with mostly white, all-American tenants, and everything looked crisp and clean. I like new, and I like clean, so I went in to speak to the manager, who turned out be rude and dismissive. Almost reluctantly, she asked me to fill out an application, When I was done, she took it without so much as glancing at it and assured me that she'd be in touch. "We have to do a credit check and all that," she explained.

Despite her hostility, I drove home in a good mood. I knew my credit was fine, and my mind was made up: That nice new building was where I wanted to live.

The next day, I called the manager to check on things, and she was more hostile than ever: "Sorry. Your credit report didn't look so hot. You've been rejected."

"How is that possible?" I asked. "I have excellent credit."

"I don't know the details," she said. "I just know what they tell me."

"Well, who ran the credit check?" I asked. "There must be some mistake." I wanted to say, *Do you know who I am? I just sold my company for $40 million, and I could buy that whole building if I wanted to*, but I bit my tongue.

"I don't know who ran the credit check," she said, sounding increasingly irked. "The head office farms that stuff out." Then she hung up on me.

I tried calling her back but she wasn't picking up and she didn't respond to my numerous messages, so I tracked down the owner of the building and told him what had happened. "I'm a very nice guy," I said. "And I don't like causing trouble. But I know that I'm not being rejected for financial reasons, and if I'm being rejected for other reasons—my appearance, say—I just want to remind you that there are laws in the State of California designed to protect people like me from discrimination."

I thought it was important to get straight to the point. There were a lot of Indians in Fremont, but that building was in a predominantly white section of town, and I got the distinct impression that the manager wanted to keep it that way.

The owner of the building asked if he could put me on hold for a moment, and within a few minutes he was back on the line. "Everything is in order," he said. "Go back and talk to her. If you want the apartment, it's yours."

The next day I went back, and she was expecting me. She was trying hard to smile, but it wasn't a particularly convincing smile. "I guess there was some mistake," she said. "You can move in on the first of the month."

"Thank you," I said.

That night I went home and told my parents about my new apartment. My mother looked numb with shock. My father betrayed no emotion whatsoever.

"Did you hear me?" I said. "I found an apartment I really like, and I'm taking it."

"We didn't think you were really going to go through with this," my mother said.

"Well, I am," I said. "I think I need to start becoming more independent."

"Your brother is three years older than you and he doesn't seem to have an issue with this," my father said.

"I'm not my brother."

By the end of the meal they were still struggling to come to terms with my decision, as if this was some kind of tragedy.

They managed to rise to the occasion. "Remember, we are always here for you," my father said, his voice void of feeling. My mother was much more emotional, but she stopped short of crying. "If it doesn't work out," she said, "this will always be your home."

I moved into the Fremont apartment a couple of weeks later, with little more than two duffel bags full of clothes, and then I went to Ikea and bought everything I thought I would need. A dresser. A bed. A desk. Lamps. A sofa. I went back three days in a row, stocking up, and I actually found it sort of enjoyable. I remember thinking *So this is real life? Interesting.*

I had everything delivered, and then I sat down and tried to put some of my purchases together. I started with the nightstand, and failed miserably. I couldn't even follow the directions, and I wasn't exactly nimble with a screwdriver. So I called the store and asked them to send someone out to help. A few days later two guys showed up and put everything together in a couple of hours. I ended up paying through the nose for their labor, so at the end of the day I hadn't really saved that much by being Mr. McFrugal.

I had to buy pots and pans and plates and put sheets on the bed and figure out how to do laundry. And I had to go shopping for food and learn how to cook some basics, which was quite a challenge for a guy who had always been served by the women in his life: grandmother, mother, sisters.

My evening meals had the feel of a science experiment. I would look at the directions and think I could double the temperature and be ready to eat twice as fast. It didn't quite work out that way, though, so I learned to follow directions. Then I bought a microwave and my life changed. Suddenly, I could cook. And I was a *good* cook. (Me and Sara Lee.) I also discovered microwavable pizza, which became a staple in my new home.

There were times, admittedly, when I was lonely, but it was a small price to pay for my freedom. I wanted to be independent, and I wanted to take responsibility for my own life, and I thought this was the way to do it. Every time I went home to visit, however, my parents and my grandmother always asked me the same thing: "When are you moving back?"

"Not today," I would reply. "I'll let you know."

Long after I was gone, they still couldn't accept it.

Even as I was trying to become a socially independent adult, however, my professional life was turning into a virtual prison. I could not get used to the corporate world. The bureaucracy. The politics. The infighting. It was nothing but noise, and it was making me very unhappy. Still, I began to realize that this was par for the course for any entrepreneur who makes the transition from his own business to working for another company, where he doesn't control things. When I was in charge, anything I wanted to do I did myself, or I asked my employees to do, and it was done precisely how I wanted it done. But in this new environment, I couldn't move forward without official approval. I had to sell an idea to one guy, then to a second guy, and then to two or three more guys after that, and they all seemed incapable of making a decision. I guess that's what people mean when they talk about the bureaucracy. It's a place where absolutely nothing gets done. And the larger the organization, the less one is able to accomplish—or so it seemed to me. It was really mind-boggling. I couldn't understand how corporations actually accomplished *anything*, since the bureaucracy seemed to be designed solely to steer you into one brick wall after another.

Still, I'm not a quitter. I have a stubborn streak that I inherited from my father, and it kept me focused. I kept telling myself that things would get better, that the people at ValueClick would eventually start listening to me and begin to turn the ship around. So I waited. And I argued. And I waited some more. And the ship held steady—on precisely the wrong course.

It was tough not being the decision maker anymore. Or, as George W. Bush has called it, the *decider.* It seemed to me that the company was being run by the accountants, which left little room for creativity. It was always about the bottom line, about the numbers; never about a vision for the future. The numbers guys couldn't think beyond profitability—which is fine, but not if it's *all* you think about. As I've already said, it's wise to keep an eye on the bottom line, but not at the expense of growing the business. When I was at the helm at Click

Agents, I was always looking ahead, thinking about where I wanted to be in a year, three years, five years—and doing everything I could to get there.

Before long, the frustration began to overwhelm me. Whenever I went home to visit—which was anytime I was in the mood for a good meal—I would bore my poor family by ranting and raving about the problems at work. "This is an Internet company. The competition is ferocious. If we don't grow, we can't compete." My parents would look at me as if I were speaking a foreign language, but they listened respectfully, and I continued to vent. "I work much better in a benevolent dictatorship." I knew my involvement with ValueClick would have to end soon. As much as it bothered me to leave the company, which I had created from scratch, I realized I would have to move on to keep my sanity.

That September, the unimaginable happened. My father called very early on the morning of the eleventh and told me to turn on the news. One tower of the World Trade Center was on fire, and I watched in horror as a plane crashed into the second. I couldn't believe what I was seeing. I sat there, open-mouthed, and watched both towers collapse. Immediately after, still in shock, I got dressed and drove over to my parents' house. We sat huddled in front of the TV, trying to make sense of what had just happened. My grandmother didn't understand what was going on—

Alzheimer's was taking a heavy toll—but my mother was terrified.

"You need to be careful out there," she said, addressing us all. "People won't understand that we are Sikhs. They will want to hurt you." Taj and I had already cut our hair and gotten rid of the turbans, so this was directed mostly at my father. But she wanted all of us to exercise caution.

In the days ahead, with the press making constant references to the Islamic terrorists, things got even worse. The average person can't be expected to tell the difference among Buddhism, Sikhism, and Islam, and our physical appearance worked against us. We had suddenly become the enemy.

One night, after a spate of violent attacks against innocent men—a gas station owner, a clerk at a 7-Eleven, etc.—the family watched a special on one of the networks. Several reporters went to great lengths to explain the differences between Arabs and Indians, between Sikhs and Muslims, and urged people not to let the situation get out of hand. This was not a religious war, they pointed out. Islam was not the enemy.

But nobody was listening. I remember running to the market with my father, to pick up a few things for dinner, and finding people turning to stare at him. They stared with undisguised hostility, teeming with hatred. I was so upset that by the time we reached the checkout line I was literally shaking, and my father could see I was on the verge of exploding.

"Say nothing," he told me in Punjabi. "You will only make it worse."

On the drive home, I was still seething. "I don't know why you put up with it," I told him.

"Because only the ignorant ones look at me like that and call me names," he replied. "And I am not going to waste my time trying to educate ignorant people. I am different and I am not afraid to be different."

Those words were a revelation to me. My father was right. I was different and I had to learn to embrace my difference. My looks, my culture, my faith—these differences had made me who I was and were shaping the man I hoped to become. Others might not know who I was, but I did—and that was enough for me.

# From Bollywood to BlueLithium

Toward the end of 2001, I was having dinner with my friend Troy at Dave & Buster's, a popular restaurant/arcade, when I noticed a pretty blonde at the bar. I kept looking over at her, and Troy kept urging me to get up and say hello. She had a friend with her, but her friend was busy talking to a guy, and the blonde seemed a little lonely. Still, I couldn't bring myself to approach her.

"What's the worst that could happen?" Troy said.

"She tells me to get lost."

"So what? There isn't a guy in the world who hasn't been told to get lost a dozen times in his life."

"I can't do it."

"G, you've told me yourself that 'Every success has its failures.' You're not going to get anywhere without trying."

He had a point. I took a sip of vodka, took a deep breath, and marched over, and in the course of the next few minutes I managed to stumble my way through every platitude in the book. "Hey, how you doing? What's your name? You alone? You come here often?" Somehow, probably because she was a little hammered, we managed to have a three-minute conver-

*With Troy Baloca at the Click Agents offices.*

sation, at the end of which she actually gave me her phone number. I returned to the table, walking on air. I couldn't believe it had worked.

"Wait two days, then call and ask her out," Troy suggested.

Two days later, I called, and we agreed to meet for dinner the next night, at Dave & Buster's, familiar ground. On the way over to her house I went into a panic. I called Troy and told him I had no idea what we were going to talk about. "What are the top ten questions for making conversation with a girl?" I asked.

"Are you kidding me?"

"No, man! I'm serious. I need help."

"Ask her what she does for a living. What she does for fun. If she likes traveling. If she has hobbies. What her family's like."

"You're going too fast!" I said.

"What? You're writing this down?"

"I was trying."

"Jesus. Then what? You're going to palm your little crib sheet and steal looks at it at the dinner table?"

He had a point. "Okay. I get it. I'll try to remember. What else?"

"Just be interested in her. People love it when you're interested in them."

It wasn't a great night. I was *too* interested. When she said she liked going to the beach, I said, "That's great! I like beaches too." And when she said she enjoyed yoga, I said I'd been interested in yoga my whole life—that, as an Indian, yoga was in my blood.

Whenever I asked her a question, she was kind enough to answer it, but I was so focused on preparing the next question that I wasn't listening, and sometimes I asked the same question twice. And when I ran out of things to ask, the silence felt interminable.

"How's that burger tasting?"

As things continued to deteriorate, I got so nervous that my hands shook when I reached for my glass. She was kind enough to *pretend* not to notice.

After dinner, I walked her to her car and said good-bye. "Call me," she said, but it was clear she didn't mean it.

I phoned Troy on my way home and gave him a blow by blow. "I'm a total loser," I said.

"I'm sure it wasn't that bad," he said.

"It was. Trust me."

"Maybe you're wrong, G. Give her a call in a couple of days and see what happens."

I called her two days later, in the middle of the day, knowing she'd be at work—I didn't have the guts to actually talk to her—and left a message. "Hey. It's Gurbaksh. Give me a call some time. If you want."

She never called, and I remember thinking that dating was a lot tougher than it looked. It had been easier to start a company than to take a woman to dinner. Then again, I was new to this. I'd never had a relationship with a woman. I didn't even know what a relationship was supposed to be. I hadn't gone to the senior prom; I left high school years two short of graduation. But even if I had stayed in school, I'm not sure I would have found a girl who was willing to go with me.

Several weeks later, still recovering, I was at an Indian restaurant with my brother, in Fremont, when I noticed two Indian girls at a nearby table, nearing the end of dinner. One got a call on her cell phone and a moment later she left in a hurry, but the friend stayed behind to finish her meal. "I think I'm going to go talk to that girl," I told my brother. He glanced over at her and said nothing. He didn't have much experience with women either. I took a deep breath, got to my feet, and went over and introduced myself.

Three days later, I was sitting across from her at a small, corner table at an Italian restaurant. We had a very nice time at dinner and started seeing each other regularly, and before long I understood what all the fuss was about. Women were great! Everything I had heard, and more! Now I knew what happened off-screen, after the Bollywood directors cut from those near-kisses to the wild, musical numbers. Suddenly the musical numbers actually made sense.

Unfortunately, the relationship didn't last. It was mostly me. I worked five and six days a week, and I was constantly flying to and from Los Angeles. Despite my problems with the brass at ValueClick, I was still determined to make good things happen. I tried to explain this to her, but she didn't seem to understand, and eventually we went our separate ways.

This business of living was certainly confusing.

That February, 2002, I finally decided to leave ValueClick. I told Sam that I was tired of trying to make myself heard and that the last couple of years had been a real disappointment for me. "I'm heavily invested in this company, and I've been trying desperately to make things happen, but nobody is really interested in what I have to say and nobody seems to give a damn about making this a more successful place."

Sam argued with me. He said I was impatient—that things didn't always move as quickly as one liked—and he asked me to stick around for another six months.

"What for?" I said. "You don't need me. I'm absolutely useless to you. I walk into the office every morning and wonder why I'm there."

"We need you, G," he said. "You are critical to the success of this operation." Really? That was news to me. "This company doesn't seem particularly interested in success," I told Sam. "And it's not from lack of trying on my part."

"Give us two months," he said. "Things will change."

Two months later, with no changes having been made, I was gone. The following week, I cashed out a portion of my shares, drove over to the Lexus dealership, and bought an SUV RX400 and a GS400 sedan. "I need these delivered tonight," I said. "Is that doable?"

"Yes sir," came the reply. "Absolutely."

I stopped by the dealership that evening and the two cars followed me to my parents' home. Both vehicles had been decked out with red ribbons, just like in the television commercials. We pulled up and I rang the bell and asked my parents to step outside. "These are for you," I said, gesturing like a game-show host.

They looked at the vehicles. Back at me. At the vehicles again. It wasn't computing.

"For us?" my father said.

"Yes. For you. For being such great parents."

My mother couldn't believe it. She shook her head from side to side, visibly disturbed. "But, Gurbaksh, we can't accept this. You need to save your money for a rainy day."

"I think I can cover a few rainy days," I replied.

"But you don't even have a job," my father protested.

"Dad, please. Take the cars for a spin."

Almost reluctantly, they got into their respective vehicles and drove to the end of the block and back. Both of them were grinning when they got out. "It is the best car I have ever driven," my father said. And I'm sure it was. In our family, whenever we saw a Lexus, we would point it out. Lexus, to us, was the epitome of perfection.

"How much will this be costing you each month?" my mother asked.

"Mom," I said, "I paid cash."

"Gurbaksh," she said. "How is this possible?"

A few months later, I contacted the title company that held the mortgage on their house. It was a thirty-year mortgage, and they had twenty-eight years to go, but their anniversary was coming up, and I wanted to surprise them. Within forty-eight hours, I had wired the money to the bank, and my parents suddenly owned their home.

"This we definitely cannot accept!" my father said.

"Too late!" I said.

"But you are going to spend all your money on us," my mother protested. "You need to be more careful. We are doing fine. Really."

And the fact is, they *were* doing fine—my father was well satisfied at the post office, and my mother enjoyed working as a nurse—but I wanted more for them. I wanted them to have the life they had dreamed of having when they left India for America.

Certainly, it was a little awkward for them, having me shower them with presents. But it gave me pleasure. It made me feel *great*, actually. And one of the lessons I took from the experience is that giving—genuine giving, giving from the heart—is way more satisfying than receiving. I would look into their eyes and I could see that they felt it was too much, but I could also see how much it meant to them. And beyond the emotional component, of course, was the simple fact that it made their lives easier. In addition, they no longer had to worry about Taj and Kamal, both of whom had become wealthy as a result of the merger. As for Nirmal, she was off in Utah with her husband, awaiting the birth of her second child, and her life seemed in order too.

Still, when all is said and done, money *does* change things, and it was no different for us. My success had a huge effect on family dynamics. I had made good in America, was living the dream that had eluded my father, and in some ways I began to usurp his role as the Chahal patriarch. I was the youngest, but I had become the one everyone turned to for answers, and it was quite the transition. As the youngest child, no one had ever asked for my opinion. In fact, on many occasions I was told, specifically, that my opinion counted for nothing. Now they wanted my opinion on almost everything. Should grand-mother have surgery? What kind of carpeting will look best in the master bedroom? Are we going to get the family together for the summer this year? I was consulted on decisions large and small, and I quite enjoyed it. It gave me something to do. After all, I was unemployed, with a full year left on my non-compete agreement, and I had so much leisure time on my hands that it was driving me crazy.

It was during this extended period of unemployment that I woke up in my Fremont apartment one morning and real-ized, perhaps for the first time, that I was really rich. I decided to do something crazy and spectacular for myself, so I bought a Lamborghini. As a kid, I had been a big fan of those Hot Wheels cars, which my parents used to find, on sale, at Toys R Us, and my very favorite was the Lamborghini, with the scis-sor doors that opened upward. Now that I had money, I thought it would be cool to own the real thing.

There were no Lamborghini dealerships in San Jose, and I didn't feel like driving to Palo Alto, so I went onto eBay Mo-tors and found one online. It was a silky gray Diablo GT Roadster Millennium Edition, only ten of which had ever been made, and it cost me $240,000, plus a little more to have it shipped to Fremont in a truck. The night before it arrived, I couldn't sleep. I couldn't stop thinking about my new car. I was going to have my very own Lamborghini. A *real* Lamborghini, not the Hot Wheels version! Whenever I managed to drift off for an hour or two, I would dream about my new car, and when I jumped out of bed in the morning I immediately called the truck driver. "Are you still on schedule?" I asked.

"Yes," he said. "I'll be there right around two o'clock."

An hour later I called again. "No delays?" I asked.

"No delays."

"Any bad weather ahead?"

"Not that I know of."

"So you'll be here at two o'clock?"

"That's what I told you an hour ago, and nothing has changed."

Sure enough, he showed up right at two, and I ran outside to greet him, as excited as a ten-year-old. He was a little surprised to see I was so young, but he went about his business, quietly and efficiently, and at long last the car was sitting on the street in front of the apartment complex, gleaming. I noticed several people on the far sidewalk standing and staring, and I must admit, somewhat shamefully, that I was filled with pride. A Lamborghini isn't something you see every day, certainly not in this neighborhood, and mine was a real knockout.

"Wow," I said. I couldn't believe it. I approached the car tentatively and opened the door. I studied the interior and inhaled that new car smell. The car smelled expensive and powerful. Then I noticed an extra pedal next to the brake. "What's that?" I asked the truck driver.

"What?"

"That pedal next to the brake?"

"That's what they call a 'clutch,'" he said.

"Clutch? Don't tell me that. That's not possible. I don't know how to drive a car with a clutch. I can only drive an automatic."

"I'm sorry to hear that, pal."

By this time, I had signed for the car, and he was ready to leave, but I begged him to help me out, and I offered him $200 to spend an hour with me and teach me how to use the clutch.

"I can't teach you in an hour," he said.

"Don't worry," I said. "I'm a fast learner."

He agreed, somewhat reluctantly, and he got behind the wheel and we began tooling around the neighborhood. He showed me how it was done: You engage the clutch, shift into the next highest gear, release the clutch, and give it some gas.

As I watched, I found myself remembering my very first driving lesson, back when I was sixteen. My sister Kamal had a small, secondhand car, which got her to and from Kaiser Permanente, where she worked as a nurse, and one day I asked her if she would teach me how to drive. She took me to a quiet, residential neighborhood and let me get behind the wheel. "That's the gas. The pedal to the left is the brake. This is where you put the car into gear. Put it in D for drive."

I started moving, but she immediately went into a panic and gave me an earful in a glass-shattering voice: "Watch out! Do this! Do that! Slow down!"

About a minute into it, I pulled over and told her to take the wheel. "I can't drive with you screaming at me," I said.

"I'm sorry," she said, calming down. "This is my motherly side. And you're my little brother. And I don't want anything to happen to you."

"Forget it. I don't want you to teach me anymore."

We swapped places and rode home in silence.

The following week I approached my father and asked for his help, and the next day he took me out in his car. I got behind the wheel and took a few careful turns around the neighborhood, and in a matter of minutes he was directing me onto the freeway. It was an incredible rush. I was doing fifty, sixty miles an hour, and cars were whizzing past me. "Oh my God," I said. "I'm driving!"

"I wouldn't go that far," he joked.

"This is amazing!"

"If you want to teach someone to swim, the trick is to throw him into the water," he said.

Over the course of the next two weeks, he took me driving a few more times. I kept improving, but I couldn't parallel park to save my life, and I can't parallel park to this day. That was my downfall when I went to take my driving test in San Jose—that damn parallel parking. But a week later I tried again, at the DMV in Gilroy, because I'd heard that they usually didn't ask you to do any parallel parking, which turned out to be the case. I actually passed the driving test. I was stunned. For the next few days, I kept taking my wallet out of my pocket to admire my learner's permit.

Now here I was, just a few years later, getting behind the wheel of my very own Lamborghini, learning how to use a clutch with the help of a very accommodating stranger. By the end of the hour, I could drive a stick shift. I felt like a total badass.

As soon as the driver left, I got into my Lamborghini and began cruising around the neighborhood. Every time I shifted, the car made a crazy grinding noise, and I could smell something burning, but I figured it was all part of the sports car experience. Also, because it was low to the ground, I kept whacking the front end, but I couldn't figure out how to avoid that.

Everywhere I went, people turned to stare, and I didn't mind it so much. I also got a lot of big, seductive smiles from pretty girls, but something told me that these weren't the types of girls I should be pursuing.

A week later I was out on the freeway, in midshift, when the Lambo died on me.

I found a mechanic in Gilroy who specialized in high-end sports cars, and he arrived half an hour later in a shiny tow truck. "I can't believe this," I whined. "I spent a ton of money on this car, and it just stopped dead."

"What have you been doing?" he asked.

"Nothing. Just driving around."

We went back to his shop in Gilroy and he took a closer look, then sauntered over to break the bad news. "Well, the front end is pretty banged up, but that's the least of it," he said. "You burned out the clutch."

At that point, it became clear to me that the grinding noise and the burning smell were not supposed to be part of the Lamborghini experience. "I'll be honest with you," I said. "I don't know how to drive this car."

The guy couldn't have been nicer. He took another Lamborghini out of the shop and we went for a drive, and before long I found out that I was supposed to take my foot off the accelerator when I was shifting gears. The experience cost me $30,000, plus a modest sum for the driving lesson.

The car continued to get a lot of attention. From time to time I'd find a handwritten note tucked under the windshield wiper from one woman or another, urging me to call. I guess they thought I was a wonderfully charismatic guy and a brilliant conversationalist, based on the car I drove, but I never phoned.

My favorite experience happened one Saturday morning as I pulled into the gym. There was a little Honda behind me, and I noticed that it had been following me for several blocks. As soon I parked and cut the engine, the Honda pulled up next to me and a kid of about sixteen got out. He looked at me with great admiration, and seemed on the verge of tears. "Oh, man," he said. "I really, really hate to bother you, but I need to know what you do for a living, because I want to get me one of those."

"I'm in Internet advertising," I said. "But that might not be for you. Just find something you love and do it better than everyone else."

Eventually I got tired of the Lamborghini and sold it on eBay, losing a few bucks in the process. I bought a Mercedes-Benz SL55. It was an automatic, and it was fast, and I loved it. Some months later, however, I began to miss my Lamborghini, so I bought another one, a red one this time, also on eBay. The following year I sold that, too, and went out to buy a Ferrari, since I'd heard so many good things about them. I went to a dealership in Los Gatos. I half expected the guys to treat me like a kid, but they were very respectful because they were selling Ferraris every day, mostly to young, dot-com millionaires. I drove off the lot in a 360 Spider, which was much easier to drive than the Lamborghini, and in fact it felt like a more solid car (but I still think the Lamborghini is way cooler). Even so, I sold the Ferrari after six months—I had only put 425 miles on it—and bought myself a white, two-door Bentley, which is what I drive to this day. It's perfect for me. It's luxurious, it's sporty, and it's easy to drive because it's an automatic.

But it's a funny thing: At one point, I thought I was getting a little carried away, and I wondered whether I was losing control of my money. But every single time I bought a car, I almost instantly had buyer's remorse. It was as if I had this built-in barometer that would go off the charts when I did anything too extravagant, and then I'd wallow in it, wondering why the hell I had done it. I was breaking one of my own business rules: *need versus necessity*. Did I really need that kind of luxury? No. Then again, maybe I'd earned it. So I lived with it. After all, as they say, *All work and no play makes G a dull boy*. But I *still* freak out a little when I spend big money, and at the end of the day I consider that a *good* thing. For example, when I fly, I fly economy. On the rare occasion when I treat myself to first class, I don't enjoy it because I can't believe I spent that much money on a ticket.

When I wasn't buying and selling cars, or dating, or polishing my game, I found something else to occupy my time: the stock market. I still had that year left on my three-year, noncompete agreement with ValueClick, so I decided to play the market with $250,000 and see what I could do with it. I got off to a great start. On my first day of trading, I made thirty grand. On the second, ten. On the third day, I was up another fifteen. I had made 20 percent on my money in three days. I was impressed with myself. I was *good*.

The next day, I started losing money. And I kept losing money. And in no time at all my original quarter million was down to $125,000. I spent months trying to get my money back. Eventually I made some trades on margin and got close to breaking.even, at which point I quit. I realized I didn't have the heart for gambling. I didn't have the stomach for it. I didn't like not being in control. So I gave it up. Another lesson learned: Leave the stock market to the professionals.

Don't get me wrong: I had studied the market pretty extensively, especially during those early years, sitting in front of the TV with my father. But it isn't who I was. I was an entrepreneur at heart. The market wasn't in my blood. And I will tell you this: You need to know what you're all about if you want to succeed. You need to play to your strengths, otherwise you're going to settle for mediocrity—and mediocrity doesn't cut it. I'm not interested in second or third place. When I play, I play to win. And anyone who can't do that doesn't belong in the game. They're not going to win with that attitude. Anybody can be good; few people can be great.

Still bored, and still looking for something to fill the hours before my noncompete expired, I decided that it would be very cool to open an Indian restaurant. I talked to Taj about it, suggesting it would be a nice way to give back to the community. "It'll be a cool place with a great vibe, a place of their own," I said. "And we can call it Planet Bollywood. Bollywood with a B."

Just about every Indian you'll ever meet is infatuated with Bollywood films, and in fact the Indian film industry is one of the largest in the world. The most popular Bollywood films are musicals, and they are full of rousing song-and-dance numbers. These were the films I used to watch with my family as a child, and I still remember many of them. Love stories and comedies and thrillers, all of them propelled along by entertaining musical numbers, which always came along at *exactly the right moment*. I remember my father once telling me that people referred to the best of these films as *paisa vasool*, which means, literally, "money's worth." I told my brother that we would create a restaurant that gave the Indian population its *paisa vasool* and then some. We wouldn't be making movies, of course, but we would serve food and drink and create a place where people could mingle and relax and have fun.

We began looking around for a viable location and found a space in nearby Milpitas. It was a French restaurant, but the owners had put it up for sale. We bought it and got ready to convert it, and I suggested that we serve French cuisine along with Indian cuisine. "A lot of Indians get Indian food at home," I said. "Maybe they're sick of Indian food."

"Sounds good to me," my brother said.

We hired contractors and designers and had to apply for permits, and six months later, with the hiring of two outstanding chefs, we had a big launch party. It was a huge success, and I felt like a real restaurateur. In fact, I felt like Rick in *Casablanca*. I went around greeting people and making sure they were enjoying themselves, and I liked the fact that everyone knew who I was. I was the Click Agents kid, the $40-million man (though it was closer to $20 million at this point). All night long, Taj and I greeted well-wishers. We were happy. We thought we were doing something wonderful for the community.

And it turned out pretty good for me, too. One night I met a gorgeous Indian girl at the restaurant, and we started dating. Many of the women who left notes on my windshield, or smiled at me at traffic lights, or approached me at the restaurant were attracted to my wealth, so I tended to be very cautious—sometimes to the point of paranoia. But this woman seemed to like me for all the right reasons.

I also made new friends at the restaurant, people from the community, people from families like my own. One of these was Krishna Subramanian, who was on the fast track to medical school. It wasn't what he wanted to do—he was an accomplished Web designer, and he loved anything to do with computers—but he was forging ahead to make his parents happy. He was definitely waffling, though. "If you ever start another company," he told me, "think of me."

"Your family would kill me," I said.

"Think of me anyway," he said.

There was one aspect of the restaurant business that I definitely didn't like: Strangers wanted things from me. Credit. Comped meals. *Loans.* Some of them tended to approach me as if I somehow *owed* them these things. One Saturday night, in the lounge, one of the more obnoxious patrons, a regular, became abusive, insulting me and demanding free drinks. When he got out of control, I had to have him booted out, and as the bouncer dragged him away he threatened to kill me. I wondered if it had been a good idea to be such a visible, high-profile owner, but I didn't let the threat bother me. The man was drunk. It was just liquor talking. (That's what I told myself, anyway.)

When my parents found out about the incident, however, they were less sanguine. They wanted me to report the man to the police, but I didn't see the point. A drunk had made an empty threat. What could the police do for me?

Amazing as it seems, Planet Bollywood had been profitable from the very start, which is almost unheard of in the

restaurant business, so it was painful to watch things deteriorate. A number of the patrons came in only to get drunk,
and it seemed as if fights broke out every weekend. These
people drained the joy from the place, and they ruined it for
everyone. Taj and I had opened the restaurant with the best
intentions, almost as a service to the Indian community, and
a handful of unpleasant people seemed determined to make
us fail.

When I spoke to my father about it, he repeated what he
had told me years earlier: "Some people are like crabs. If they
can't get over the wall, they will pull you down to keep you
from climbing over."

I was also reminded of something I'd once heard said by
Simon Cowell, one of the judges on *American Idol*. He
claimed that he found it depressing whenever any of his
friends succeeded; the interviewer laughed, thinking he was
kidding. But Simon wasn't kidding at all. He *hated* to see his
fellow crabs making it over the wall.

I also heard a famous quote on the subject, attributed to
author Gore Vidal: "It's not enough to succeed; others must
fail."

I don't understand that kind of thinking. I'm not like that.
When I see someone succeed, I find it inspiring. I'm not jealous. I'm not resentful. On the contrary, I figure if they can do
it, I can do it too. But some people seem to resent success in

others, and it was clear that I wasn't about to change their thinking.

Unhappy with the way things continued to deteriorate at Planet Bollywood, I looked for other ways to occupy my time, and at one point I flew to San Jose, Costa Rica, to meet with the owners of a Korean-based software firm. They had expressed an interest in working with me, and for the next few months I flew back and forth between the two San Joses, trying to help them get their company off the ground.

While this was going on, I got a call from Sam, back at ValueClick, who was eager to talk business. "You are the second largest shareholder in the company," he said. "The only person who has more shares than you is the founder. You have more shares than *I* do. We were wondering if you might want to sell your stock to us. We'd be willing to buy you out for cash."

This sounded a little suspect. When the shares were at $7.50, they had been worth $40 million. At $2.50, they had lost two-thirds of their value. Sam offered me $3 a share, which didn't seem particularly generous, but I told him I'd think about it. Before I did anything, however, I wanted more information on what the company had been up to lately. I'd been out of the loop for a year, so I was in the dark about recent developments. Sam said he didn't have a problem with that; he'd put something in the mail to me and send me the relevant information as soon as I signed. In a matter of days, I received a document stating that ValueClick intended to buy all of my stock at $3 a share but that nothing would move forward until I'd received the requested information on the company's near-term goals. It was a nonbinding agreement, and the document talked only about the *proposed* sale, so I went ahead and signed it.

One Sunday night, I returned home from yet another trip to Costa Rica and fell to bed exhausted. Just before eight the following morning, my phone rang. It was my brother, and he was in a panic. "Get over to the restaurant right now!" he said.

"Dude," I said, still only half awake. "I got in late last night after a long-ass flight from Costa Rica. I'm beat."

"The restaurant is on fire," he said.

I jumped out of bed, dressed in a hurry, and raced over, and I arrived to find the place engulfed in flames. Fire engines were everywhere, but the firemen were fighting a losing battle. The restaurant looked as if it had been bombed, and it appeared deliberate.

In the days ahead, we talked to the fire department and to the police, and from everything we saw and heard it looked like a case of arson. But they had nothing to go on, so they did nothing. That's when we started hearing the rumors. People in the Indian community—my own people—were saying that the restaurant had turned out to be a bad investment and that we had burned it down for the insurance money. They were wrong on both counts. The restaurant had been a very good investment, but it had attracted the wrong crowd, and after only four months it was all over. And we didn't have enough insurance to cover a fraction of what we had put into it. In fact, we lost a small fortune on the venture. Still, the rumors persisted, and there was absolutely nothing we could do to dispel them.

The idea that people in our own community, fellow Indians, would think we could be so dishonest was very upsetting to us both. Our intentions had never been anything less than honorable.

My brother and I went to talk to the arson unit again, begging them to investigate, but they said they had already tried. "We couldn't find anything," they said. "It certainly looks like arson, but maybe it's not arson. Maybe it was just a freak accident."

For weeks afterward, in my own neighborhood, at the coffee shop, at the grocery store, I would find people smiling at me conspiratorially, as if I'd gotten away with burning down my restaurant. Again, *these were my own people*. What part of this didn't they understand? Even if the place had been fully insured, which it wasn't, the restaurant was not and never had been about the money. I had been trying to do something for the community, and clearly that had been a big mistake. It taught me yet another lesson: Forget noble motivations. Pursue your own interests and focus on making yourself happy. That's what I'd done with Click Agents, and I had made myself very happy indeed. I had also made a lot of other people happy, people who had worked hard to make the company a success. Many of them would never have to work another day in their lives, and that had nothing to do with noble intentions. I had pursued my dreams and others had shared in my success.

After the fire, I went into a funk. For a while, I felt completely lost. I was an entrepreneur, and I missed exercising that talent. I didn't know what to do with myself, so I was restless and unfocused and probably more than a little irritable, and my parents became deeply concerned. "Why don't you go back to school?" my father said. "It's been three years since you dropped out, and you're very close to getting your high school diploma."

"What's the point?" I said. "It feels like a giant backward step."

"The point? The point is this: One day you will have kids of your own, and they will give you trouble. 'My dad doesn't have a high school degree and look at him! Why should I pay attention in school? I want to be a dropout, like him.'"

Okay. Point taken. A few weeks later, I found myself scrambling to complete my high school requirements while taking a slew of new courses at San Jose State. I tried to be optimistic. I told myself that experience might lead to something new and exciting.

One day an Indian girl approached me after class. "You're Gurbaksh Chahal, aren't you? The restaurant owner."

"Yes," I said.

"I hear you burned the place down for the insurance money."

Man, it was all I could do not to explode. I tried to count to ten, but I only got as far as five. "Listen to me," I said. "I don't know who told you that story, but it's bullshit. If you want to know the truth, I'm a cheap bastard, and I was grossly underinsured. I got $100,000 from the insurance company. That's it. And after paying off my debts and the lawyers, I was left with nothing. Zip. Zero. I put a million dollars of my own money into that place, and I lost every penny of it."

I guess my outburst startled her a little. "I'm sorry," she said.

"You should be," I said, and I stormed off.

Two weeks later, I dropped out of school for a second time. It was boring. Nothing about it was remotely interesting to me. And you know, I'm probably going to be taken to task for this, but I have no regrets about dropping out—not the first time and not that second time. I am sure I would have learned plenty in school; I might have even learned a few things that would have helped me make smarter, more in-formed decisions; but I'm just not a textbook kind of guy. And sure, there are things I don't know—I don't know much about art or literature—but if and when the time comes, I can pur-sue those interests on my own. So no: absolutely no regrets. Maybe in the early part of my adventures other people would have been more comfortable if I'd had a degree—the stereo-types, remember?—but a degree wouldn't have made real dif-ference in my life.

I went back to my apartment in Fremont and waited for my noncompete agreement to expire. As I began to think about my next venture, I made a horrendous discovery: The team at ValueClick had purchased the balance of my shares at $3 a share, transferred them out of my account, and left me with the proceeds from the sale. This was bad enough, but it was only the beginning: Right on the heels of that transaction, *the price of the stock began to climb*. I didn't understand it. I had signed an agreement in which I agreed to the *possibility* of sell-ing my shares back to the company, but somebody had jumped the gun. Clearly this was a mistake. Was it possible the mistake had been mine?

I called Sam to find out what was going on, but I didn't hear back from him, and I kept calling without success. He ig-nored both my calls and my e-mails.

In a matter of months, ValueClick hit $8 a share, and I was completely dumbfounded. Since I wasn't getting answers from Sam and the team, I hired a lawyer and sued them for securities fraud. I was the second largest shareholder in the company, and the company had a fiduciary responsibility to me. Even if the mistake had been mine, the situation didn't add up. As you might imagine, the whole thing was incredibly depressing. Every time the stock went up a point, I despaired a little more.

My father tried to comfort me, quoting from a scripture: "Hatred finds a place in hell; forgiveness is where He is."

A month later, while the lawyers were still battling it out, I left Fremont and took a high-end apartment in Santana Row, an upscale development just outside San Jose. The area had dozens of restaurants and bars and chic stores, and I liked the fact that I could walk to all of them.

I spent Christmas with my family, as always. Christmas is not a Sikh tradition, but we celebrate in our own small way. When I was younger, we'd save our money and our parents would drive us to McFrugal's or to the 99-cent store, and we'd buy presents for each other—presents that actually meant something. A little teacup for my mother, say. Or a pocket comb for my father's flowing beard. I was older now, and I could afford more, but I still put plenty of thought into the presents. My dad got a Rolex. My mother got several cash-mere sweaters. And my grandmother got a beautiful cane because she was having trouble walking. She was deteriorating in other ways, too. By this point, she was so physically weak that she'd sit at the table, immobile, and we had to remind her to eat. It was painful for me. I thought back to the way she had comforted us as kids, and I wanted to do the same for her: I wanted to tell her that everything was going to be okay, but of course it wasn't going to be okay, and it broke my heart. This was the woman who had hidden my bad report cards from my parents, who had let me sleep in her bed when I was afraid of the boogeyman, who had comforted me when I was reluctant to go to my own parents for comforting, and Alzheimer's was slowly and surely turning her into a stranger. She was the pillar of the Chahal family, so it was the one sour note in an otherwise pleasant Christmas.

As 2003 got under way, Taj and I decided to buy some property. He was still living at home and figured it was time to move out, and much as I loved my Santana Row apartment I was throwing my money away on rent.

We went to look at a couple of houses at The Ranch on Silver Creek, an upscale country club development on the outskirts of San Jose, and ended up buying unfinished homes right next to each other. For the next six months I spent a lot of time and money fixing up my place. It was a 5,000-square-foot house, and I installed built-ins, and miles of marble, and a state-of-the-art sound system. Every room in the house was wired, including the bathrooms. But whenever I was over there, checking on the workmen, I would look out at the sweeping, golf course views and wonder what I'd been thinking. I didn't play golf and I had no interest in playing golf. The whole place—the *idea* of the place—was way too Zen for me. I like action and adrenaline, and golf seemed to be the antithesis of that.

During this period I started dating again and met a few interesting women, but nothing serious developed. Part of it was my problem, admittedly. Most of the women knew who I was, and it was hard to tell whether their interest was genuine. I think I erred on the side of paranoia.

I had similar problems with friends. I was close to guys like Troy and Krishna, who wanted nothing from me except friendship, but a lot of other people seemed to be forever on the make. They wanted a deal or a job or a loan or a free dinner. Regarding the dinner business, these lesser friends always stuck me with the tab. The check would arrive, and they'd sit there as if they'd suddenly lost the use of their arms, and I'd find myself reaching for my credit card. I understood their thinking, of course—they figured a day's worth of interest on my money added up to more than I could spend in a month— but that wasn't the point. It would have been nice if they had reached for the tab from time to time, if only as a gesture, but they never did, and I eventually stopped seeing them. I take friendship seriously, and I have since learned how to spend my time wisely surrounded only by genuine people. It's funny, because I'd already learned this lesson—the notion that you need to surround yourself with people who want you to succeed—but I couldn't always put it into practice. I like people. I like having friends. And sometimes I'm a little too forgiving. But at the end of the day I had to learn to watch my back, because sometimes staying on top is harder than getting there. Never lose sight of the definition and presence of the word "real."

Later that same year I discovered Las Vegas. Troy was about to get married, and he had his bachelor party in Sin City. I was among the half dozen friends he asked along, and I fell in love with the place almost immediately. I liked the energy. I liked the restaurants. I liked the night life. Most of all, I liked the anonymity. Back in San Jose, where information was only a mouse click away, people knew way too much about me, most of it wrong. But in Vegas, where I didn't even have to share my name, I could be whoever I wanted to be.

The funny thing is, when I first started going to Vegas, I felt like a kid in a candy store. Before long I figured it out: I hadn't really had much of an adolescence; I was having fun for the first time in my life. But in time I realized there was another component, and that's this: Vegas is a culture where identity doesn't really matter. You can be whomever you want to be. You can even be nobody—it's a level playing field—and sometimes being nobody is a pretty good thing.

In October, Taj and I went to Maui for Troy's wedding. We stayed at the Grand Hyatt Wailea, which was pretty plush. There were a lot of honeymooning couples around and not a single girl anywhere in sight, but Taj and I made the most of it. We partied with the other guests, ate well, and slept with the windows wide open, listening to the surf and enjoying the ocean breezes.

The day before the wedding, Troy came up to me and said, "I'm nervous about my speech. How's your speech coming?"

"Speech?" I said. "What are you talking about?"

And he said, "Dude, you're the best man. You're supposed to give a speech."

"I thought I was supposed to hand you the rings. You didn't say anything about a speech."

"It's traditional, man!"

"Not in India," I replied.

Now he was doubly nervous. He was nervous about his speech and even more nervous about my nonspeech. But I told him not to worry. I'd work something out.

After he left, I sat down and made a few notes about Troy and about our friendship, and for the rest of the day I was in a state of anxiety. The ceremony took place outdoors, within view of the beach, in front of about fifty people, and I was probably more nervous than Troy. When it was time, I got to my feet and looked at the expectant crowd, all of whom were clearly waiting to be wowed by humor, heartfelt words, and wisdom. I was reminded of my speech at Accel some years earlier, on Viagra, and I thought that that was somehow appropriate, given that this was Troy's Big Night, and for a moment I thought it might be amusing to deliver that speech. But no. I took a deep breath, looked at Troy and his bride, and plunged in. I told Troy he was like a brother to me and that in marrying Zena she was becoming part of my family. "Both of you are amazing people, and when I look at you I realize that what they say is true: There are some couples who *do* complete each other.

"I am honored to be your friend. If there's anything you need, ever, anytime, you know where to find me."

I think the speech was well received. People were clapping and crying. Nobody threw anything at me. I raised my glass in a toast to the bride and groom, and the guests toasted them with me. I remember thinking that I was glad I hadn't blown it. I also remember thinking that public speaking wasn't all that hard.

My brother and I watched people dance for a couple of hours. There were a number of attractive women in the wedding party, but most of them were married, and as I watched them waltz with their significant others, I began to entertain a crazy fantasy: One day I would meet the perfect woman, and she would fall madly in love with me before she found out I was rich.

When I got back to San Jose, still entertaining that crazy fantasy, I got marginally better at approaching women in bars and restaurants, and at asking them out, and at making conversation—but I still found myself questioning their motivations. It may well have been my own paranoia, but that didn't invalidate my principal worry: Was it me they liked, or was it my money?

This was a lesson I hadn't expected to learn: Money brings huge rewards, but it also introduces you to a whole new set of problems.

That year, with my noncompete agreement close to expiring, and with my fantasy as yet unfulfilled, I began to think about getting back into the business of business, but I got sidetracked by *The Apprentice.* The show was preparing for another season on NBC, and it was looking for potential candidates. I was a businessman and an entrepreneur, and several of my friends convinced me that I was the *perfect* candidate, so I went ahead and filled out an application. I included some details about Click Agents, about my time with ValueClick, and I even cut a DVD in which I said that

I'd always been curious about Hollywood, that I liked to be challenged, and that I would welcome an opportunity to audition for the show.

A month later, I received an e-mail: "Congratulations! You are one of the finalists." Not long after, I was summoned to the Clift Hotel, in San Francisco, for a meeting with the casting department. I waited in the lobby with a number of other candidates, and at last a young woman showed up, called my name from the long list on her clipboard, and led me away. I followed her into the elevator and down a corridor, and eventually I found myself in the suite where the auditions were being held. There were two people in the room, both of whom greeted me quite effusively, and I took a seat. That's when I saw the cameraman, and I guess they noticed my discomfort.

"Any objections?"

"No," I said. "I guess not."

As soon as the camera started rolling, the questions began, and they were fairly personal in nature. Nobody had ever asked me for so much detail about my dating habits, my relationship with my parents, my friendships, my hobbies, and so on—and certainly not on camera. I was so nervous that my own voice sounded alien to me.

When it was over, the same young lady walked me back to the lobby, telling me that several thousand people had applied for a spot on the show and that only a few hundred made the cut. "You did great," she said.

I didn't believe her. After that performance, I was pretty sure I was not ready for prime time, and in short order my suspicions were confirmed: I got a very nice form letter telling me that I would not be going toe to toe with the Donald.

Some weeks later, when my noncompete finally expired, I decided to forget about show business and get back to my first love. I had a few ideas about the kind of business I wanted to start, but all I knew for sure was that it would be another ad network. Still, that was all I needed to know. Most people think they need to know *exactly* what they want to do when they start a business, but they're wrong. If you go into something with a very specific plan, you might be so focused on your goal that you won't see the promising opportunities that present themselves as you make your way along. Take the blinders off. Look around. Don't be afraid to go off on all sorts of unusual directions, since that's where you might just find the most interesting— and promising—opportunities.

I knew only two specific things about my future company: One, it would do much the same thing Click Agents had done, but it would do it better. And two, the focus would be on innovation, particularly as it related to behavioral targeting. On this latter point, I wanted to figure out what the consumer wanted, then give it to him or her, and I had some ideas on how to do that—but I wasn't there yet.

On January 12, 2004, the uncertainties notwithstanding, I launched my next company. I rehired my brother and sister, along with several of my former star employees, and settled into new offices in downtown San Jose. They were cheap, because *I'm* cheap. When it comes to spending money I always repeat that familiar mantra: need versus necessity. Do I really need a $5,000 couch in the lobby, or will a used one do? I think you know the answer to that.

But take note: Being cheap is good for the company and for the shareholders, but don't be *too* cheap. Never be cheap with your employees, for example. If one of them is a rock star, pay him or her a rock-star salary. This is very important. When staffing a company, you should always hire people who are smarter than you. I may be a dictator, but I'm a benevolent dictator, and I'm not intimidated by intelligence. On the contrary, I want people around me who are smart enough to question what I'm doing. (Within reason, of course.) I want to fill every slot in my company with the best possible candidate. Think of it this way: An orchestra conductor always hires the most talented musicians available. Why? Because when they're working together as a team, under his direction, he knows he is going to get the most magnificent possible sound. Well, that's what I wanted for my company: beautiful music.

At that point, almost reluctantly, I called my friend Krishna. Years earlier, I had promised to call him if I ever launched a new company, and I was keeping my word. Still, it was tough. He had just been accepted into medical school, and I didn't want him to get sidetracked. "I don't want to be a doctor," he said, repeating what he had told me years earlier. "I was doing this for my parents. My first love is the Internet."

Needless to say, his parents weren't very happy with me. They had their hearts set on seeing their son in medical scrubs, and they didn't understand why I had meddled in his life. I felt badly about this, of course, but Krishna was an adult, and I figured he could make up his own mind.

For the first couple of weeks, as we settled into the new offices, the company didn't even have a name, and it was getting pretty frustrating. We spent days trying to figure out what we were going to call ourselves. Anything with the word "click" was already taken, and the good domain names were either taken or for sale at exorbitant prices. Domain names, with which I'd had some experience in my youth, are something of a commodity, and companies have been known to spend a fortune on them. Computer.com, for example, sold for $8.5 million. Diamond.com sold for $10 million. Sex.com sold for $20 million. That's the nature of the beast. You spend the money because the name becomes an instant brand. It sticks. It resonates. And it takes consumers to your site.

One evening, I was out at Dave & Buster's with Taj and Krishna, still brainstorming over a damn name. We wanted it to be a little different but not *too* different. Some of the elements in the periodic table had pretty cool names, and I had brought a copy to the bar with me. Titanium. Platinum. Tungsten. Chromium.

There were names that *weren't* cool. *Helium* was laughable. *Berylium* sounded like a girl's name, but the kind of girl you wouldn't take on a second date. *Silicon*—no, that was taken by Silicon Valley. *Dubnium* sounded like the first name of a Russian mobster, and *argon* sounded like a poison in a superhero movie.

As we were sitting there, growing increasingly frustrated, the bartender came over with three shots of Hypnotic, a blue, vodka-based concoction that was the cool drink back then (at least in San Jose). As it happened, I looked down at the periodic table as the drinks arrived, and the word "lithium" seemed to jump out at me. "Blue lithium," I said out loud. From the looks on their faces, it was clear that that was the name we'd been looking for: BlueLithium. It didn't mean anything, but it sounded like it might, and—at the end of the day—it was *cool.*

Like Click Agents, BlueLithium was going to go into the business of Internet advertising, but more from the behavioral targeting end of things. Let me explain: In traditional advertising, the key to success lies, primarily, in targeting the right demographic. If you have a product to sell, you're going to want to put your ad in front of people who might actually buy it. If there's a football game on TV, for example, you're going to see commercials for beer, pizza, and rugged trucks, because clearly there are plenty of football-watching guys who like beer, pizza, and rugged trucks. An ad for an anti–wrinkle cream, though, wouldn't do well during a football game. Similarly, if you're reading *Outdoor Life* magazine, you're likely to find plenty of ads for guns and crossbows and not many ads for air fresheners or toilet bowl cleaners.

The goal for the advertiser, then, is as simple as it is self-evident: Where do I go to get the biggest return? Where am I likely to make the most sales?

That's where technology came into the picture, and it was changing every day—pretty dramatically at times. In the advertising world, it's all about making the ads more effective—about getting the right ads in front of the right eyeballs—and advertisers were beginning to figure out how to track the habits and tastes of online consumers. I'll give you an example you might be able to relate to: When you buy a book from Amazon, you might receive an e-mail from the company a week or two later, with a suggestion on *another* book, based on the book you bought, and even on the interests of other people who also bought that first book. Or if you have TiVo and you watch certain types of shows, it won't be long before the system is making suggestions about *other* shows it thinks you might enjoy. It's that simple. The computer keeps track of your tastes, creating a profile, and it starts steering you toward products and services it believes you will respond to.

It follows, then, that if an advertiser knows what a person is interested in—if the advertiser can figure out the types of sites the person is drawn to—the company will be able to target the ads more effectively. By the way, there is nothing Big Brotherish about this. The advertising companies don't know whom they are targeting, and they don't care. All they know is that a particular stranger is responding to certain types of ads, and their goal is to put those types of ads—and *only* those types of ads—in front of that stranger. I don't want to try to sell diapers to a truck driver. It's a waste of my time, and it clutters up his computer screen. I want to put an ad in front of that truck driver that has a good chance of getting his attention.

The trick, of course, boils down to figuring out how to follow people as they make their way around the Internet, to get a sense of their likes and dislikes. And to do this, I had to find an Internet company that had the right type of ad-serving system (the technology that allows you to put ads on the Web sites).

For a time, I considered going to India, where I could hire a team to build a program from scratch, but I knew that that would take the better part of a year and I didn't want to wait that long. Just as I was beginning to despair, however, I got lucky. I found an outfit called Ad Revolver. It was in the online advertising business and appeared to be making use of some rudimentary ad-serving software. I called the number in Louisiana, and from the way the phone rang I could tell I had been bounced overseas.

"Hello," said a man said with a heavy accent. He sounded Russian.

"Is this Ad Revolver?" I asked

"Yes," he said.

"I want to know about you guys."

"Who are you, and what do you want to know?"

"My name is G," I said. "I'm calling from San Jose, California, and I'm starting an Internet company. I think we might be a good fit."

Ad Revolver was located in Belarus, in the city of Minsk, but it was registered in Louisiana, which is friendly to foreigners, and, as a result, was licensed to operate in the United States. After speaking to that first gentleman, I also spoke to his brother, who happened to be his partner, and the following week they sent me a prototype of their software. I was sufficiently impressed that I decided to pursue it, and not long after we met in London.

At that point, they didn't know much about me because I hadn't told them much—not even my full name. If I had given

them my name, and they had Googled me, it would have colored the negotiations—if it ever came to that. Now, however,
with things moving forward, I was going to have to take my
chances.

We met at Le Méridien Hotel, in London's Piccadilly
Circus, and I told them who I was, what I'd done in the past,
and what I hoped to accomplish with BlueLithium. As we
talked, I did what I always do when I'm trying to assess a person's potential: I asked myself whether these two brothers had
the right DNA to join me and make things happen for my
company. A lot of people look for perfection right out of the
gate, and I think this is a big mistake. Nothing is perfect, so
for me it's really about the future and about whether I think
the candidate and I are a good fit. In this case, the answer was
a resounding yes. As for their program, it was good, but it
wasn't where it needed to be. If I had to compare it to a car,
I'd say they had a standard, assembly-line Mercedes-Benz,
whereas I was looking for the souped-up AMG version of that
same, solid vehicle. The good news was that they understood
exactly what I needed, particularly in terms of behavioral
tracking, and it became immediately clear to me that these
guys had the talent to make it happen.

When the meeting wrapped, I decided to fly to Belarus to
take a look at their operation. They were booked on a flight
that same evening, and I said I'd follow the next day.

I didn't have a visa, however, and I made some calls and learned that it would take two weeks to get one. I was also told I could take my chances and fly to Belarus without a visa, though there was no guarantee I'd be permitted to stay in the country. Deciding to take my chances, I booked a flight on Belavia Airlines. The next morning, when I took my seat on the aircraft, the seat belt didn't even work. Not exactly confidence inspiring.

We landed safely, but I ran into trouble at immigration. An armed soldier was summoned and led me into the bowels of the building, where I found myself being questioned by a man with a heavy accent.

"You not have visa?"

"No, I don't have a visa."

"Why you not have visa?"

"They said it would take two weeks to get one, and I wanted to come over right away."

"What for you in such hurry?"

"I'm meeting with two brothers who live here in Minsk. We might go into business together."

"What business?"

"Internet advertising," I said.

He studied my passport and shook his head, looking grim. Then he looked dead at me and said, "You like Madonna?"

"She's all right," I said, wary.

"Next time you come to Belarus, you bring for me Madonna CD?"

"Sure," I said. "I'll bring you a couple."

A moment later, he reached for his stamp and stamped my passport. I was in. I had my visa.

The Ad Revolver guys were waiting for me outside the terminal, along with their father, who had been enlisted to pick me up—he owned a car, they didn't. The father didn't speak much English, but on the way into the city he would tell the brothers to point out the sights. The old KGB building. The Minsk ballet. The Botanical Gardens. Victory Square. Lenin Square. And so on and so forth. The city was beautiful and very clean, and there were lots of people on the streets, but it seemed as if nobody lived there. I think it had something to do with the energy. When you go to Manhattan, the city is alive and wild. But in Minsk, everything seemed tamped down and sedated.

When we reached the hotel, they gave me a few minutes to check in and freshen up, and then they took me to a local Belarusian restaurant. It was pretty good. We had borscht, caviar, whitefish, some kind of potato pancakes with mushrooms, and several shots of vodka. I ate everything, because I only have one rule when it comes to food: If it's alive, don't eat it.

*G in Belarus with the Ad
Revolver team.*

The next morning they came to fetch me at the hotel and
drove me to their offices, which turned out to be a collection
of apartments. They had several guys working with them, and
part of their business was focused on video games. I was very
impressed with the operation. They were high-energy, low-
cost guys. I liked their style.

I asked them, "If I wanted to take the company off your
hands today, what would you want?"

They said, "Half a million dollars."

I said, "Done. But you can do better."

"How?"

"I'll give you a stake in my new company. In return, you
can be my technology department, as well as my research and
development team."

They accepted my offer, which turned out to be a very wise choice, and I flew home to begin getting the company off the ground.

I didn't know exactly where BlueLithium was going, or exactly *how* it was going to get there, but I knew instinctively that it was going to be big.

# The Art of War

**W**hen I returned from Minsk, I got busy looking for investors. I assumed that most of them would be impressed with the success of Click Agents, but I'd assumed wrong. Most of them wanted to meet, partly because they were curious about me, but I couldn't get any of them to commit any money, and several of them actually told me to come back when I was bigger. Bigger? Really? All I could think was *When I'm bigger, I won't need you.*

Some of them were downright rude. For example, one of these meetings was with a general partner at a big firm, and I was worried that he really didn't have the industry background to understand what BlueLithium was all about. He did have an MBA from an Ivy League university, however, and—as a high school dropout—I guess I was impressed.

When I arrived for the meeting, I was ushered into a conference room and kept waiting for about ten minutes. I think only insecure people keep you waiting. It's their way of telling you that they are more important than you are. When he showed up, we shook hands and made a little small talk, and then I started my PowerPoint presentation. About four minutes into it, when I was on my third slide, he asked me to stop. He was studying me with a patronizing smirk. "This isn't working for me," he said.

"Excuse me?"

"You have no focus."

Focus? I was just getting started. How could he possibly know whether I had "focus"? I bit my tongue, but it wasn't easy.

"And honestly," he went on, "I don't think you picked an area that has any growth potential."

I still said nothing.

"Listen, I am trying to do you a favor here. I want to save you a lot of time and a lot of heartache. This is not a good field. Your chances of success are pretty much zero."

For the next ten minutes, he lectured me, and I felt like I was in a classroom, listening to the basics of Business 101. Worse, the lecture was being delivered by a guy who had less experience than I did. But I still said nothing. When it was finally over, I actually thanked him for his time and for his inspiring words, and then I got the hell out of there. And, pal, if you're reading this, what do you have to say for yourself now?

There were other meetings that weren't quite as infuriating, but none of them got me to the next level. When you're looking for venture capital, the next level is the term sheet. A term sheet is a nonbinding agreement that lays out the general terms and conditions of the deal, and the financing goes through as soon as both parties have agreed to all the points. At that stage, with the term sheet signed, lawyers on both sides sit down and hammer out an actual contract, which usually takes four to six weeks. Alas, I began to think there would be no term sheet in my future, let alone an actual contract, so I resigned myself to moving forward without any financial partners.

By late March, while I still trying to find the right software for my new venture, my lawyer called to tell me that I was being sued by the team at ValueClick.

"For what?" I asked.

"They're angry because you sued them for securities fraud," my lawyer said.

"So what? It's payback time?"

"Pretty much," he said.

In their suit, ValueClick suggested I had stolen "trade secrets," but they never described the so-called secrets in any detail. And the company also accused me of trademark infringement. This latter charge stemmed from the fact that I had used the Click Agents logo on one of my Web sites, since I had founded the company, and since it made sense for me to mention it, even in passing, when I was describing my history. Still, to satisfy this claim, I immediately removed the logo, and henceforth any references to Click Agents were made in plain, unadorned type.

The most upsetting aspect of the suit, however, had nothing to do with trade secrets, with ValueClick, or with Click Agents. It didn't even have anything to do with the Internet. It was about Planet Bollywood, in fact, and about those arson allegations. The lawsuit suggested than I had been part of a police investigation, which was a complete lie and an obvious attempt to undermine my credibility. I was very sensitive about this, as I valued my reputation—it defines me as a person and as a businessman, and one must always protect it. At the same time, the reasoning was obvious: ValueClick needed to convince the judge that I was the type of guy who might steal trade secrets.

Then it occurred to me that the lawsuit might also have been designed, at least in part, to frighten off potential investors. This only made me more determined to succeed, but I was still angry—the last thing I needed was to become embroiled in nasty, time-consuming litigation. Still, I had to defend the suit, and I began to bleed money the moment I picked up the phone to call the lawyers. It felt like déjà vu all over again: I had gone through much the same thing with that London programmer, and the idea that I was going to be subjected to more of the same really infuriated me. I was particularly upset because the experience taught me that any determined person can sue anyone over anything. In some cases, when you weigh the costs of defending your principles, you discover that it makes sense to simply settle. Business people have to accept that as a reality of doing business. Still, it's deeply troubling. In most civilized countries—the United Kingdom, for example—it's completely different. If someone sues and loses, they have to pay all the legal expenses—theirs *and* yours. This happens in America too, of course, but first you have to win your case, and then you have to go back to court and sue your adversary for legal fees that you should never have incurred in the first place.

At the end of the day, it seemed that the motivation behind this suit had one aim: to ruin my chance to get BlueLithium—a potential competitor—off the ground. But I wasn't going to let that happen.

I learned several lessons from that harrowing experience. First, failure is not an option. Anyone who even entertains the idea of failure is already doomed. Whenever you set out to do something, large or small, you have to believe in your heart that it's going to happen, and you have to keep moving toward that goal. It's really all about forward movement—like riding a bicycle. If you're standing still, it's not easy to keep your balance, but if you're moving forward, there's nothing to it. That holds true for business—and for life. *So keep moving forward.*

The other lesson I learned was equally valuable: Don't get emotional. I was angry, sure. I didn't want to go through that fresh hell all over again, and I didn't want the people close to me—my brother, my sister, all my employees—to get dragged into it with me. But I am also aware that logic and emotions don't mix, and I was able to disengage emotionally. I would let the lawyers handle it. After all, that's what they were getting paid for.

And finally—a lesson that bears repeating: Learn to move on when it's time to move on. Bite the bullet. Let go. Start fresh. Don't look back. It's not as easy as it sounds, but make the effort—it's worth it.

Ironically, a private equity group from Chicago had been secretly looking at BlueLithium, and not long after the suit was filed they offered to invest $20 million to help grow the company. At the time, this came as a bit of a surprise, and it also seemed like a great deal of money. With the business just getting off the ground, I was only generating about $200,000 a month in revenue, and I wondered what they might want for that $20 million. Still, their interest gave me power and cachet, so we started talking. Before we did, however, I discussed the situation with my family, telling them that I needed to be up front with the Chicago money men about the ValueClick lawsuit. They all agreed with me, but they told me to be patient. There was a chance we might reach an early settlement, and they suggested I let that possibility play out.

The lawsuit didn't go away, however, and the Chicago investors were moving forward very quickly. I liked this—I like to make things happen, and the faster they happen the more I like it—but with no settlement in sight I decided it was time to tell them. I walked them through the whole miserable situation, and they listened politely, but it was clear that our little dalliance was over. "We don't play that game," they said. "It complicates everything."

This only made me more determined to succeed. The lesson here is simple: Don't lose your moral barometer. Lies and obfuscation might give you short-term success, but they make for very unstable relationships.

That summer I finally settled my legal problems with ValueClick and got back to the business of business. I could have stayed and fought the suit, and my lawyers felt I could have won, but they didn't think it would have been worth it. So I withdrew my suit accusing them of securities fraud, and they withdrew their suit against me, and neither of us acknowledged any wrongdoing. It was a wash.

The guys in Belarus, meanwhile, were still working on my new program. It wasn't there yet, but it showed promise. With Click Agents, I had been running a basic, pay-per-click operation, but with BlueLithium I was going to take things to a whole new level. I was still dealing with the same three constituencies—advertiser, site owner, and consumer—but I was getting better acquainted with the consumer. And it wasn't that much of a challenge. People reveal their likes and dislikes as they make their way through the Internet, moving from site to site, and it had become possible to follow them around. We didn't know the consumer's name, we didn't know his age, we didn't know where he lived—and none of that meant anything to us. What we did know, for example, is that he or she had shown interest in the Four Seasons hotel chain, and we could then "tag" that person with a "cookie" and follow him around the Web, enticing him with more ads for the Four Seasons or with ads that appealed to Four Seasons' kind of people.

In effect, BlueLithium was poised to disrupt the Internet advertising model. We were saying "I can find you on the Internet based on your behavior." It didn't matter whether you were on CNN.com or MySpace or visiting *The New York Times* online, we were able to find you because we had behavioral data that told us where you'd been and where you might be going. And when we found you, we would entice you with all the right ads. (That was the idea, anyway.)

At this point, even before we'd launched the new technology, our revenues had exceeded our wildest expectations, and I began to think that I should give the venture capital route another try. I didn't need the money at the time, but I knew that BlueLithium was going to be much larger than Click Agents, and I wanted to have the funds in place when it came time to make expensive decisions.

I made a few calls, exploring the possibilities, and the next thing I knew I heard from a reporter at *VentureWire*. *VentureWire* is part of the Dow Jones financial information service, and it is read by just about everyone in the investor community, and usually it gets things right—but not this time. "I hear you're about to finalize a $10 million round of funding," the reporter said. No, I said, correcting him. I was in the *process* of raising $10 million, and things were moving in that direction, but nothing had been finalized.

As soon as this nonnews hit the wires, my phone started ringing, and every single venture capital guy was asking me the same question: "Can we jump in?" There was a tremendous sense of urgency—they all wanted a piece of BlueLithium— and all because they thought they had competition.

As a result, I was able to take my pick from a number of viable investors, and I narrowed it down to two candidates: Walden VC and 3i.

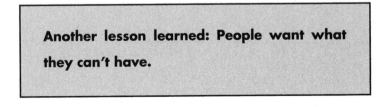

**Another lesson learned: People want what they can't have.**

Generally, you have a lead investor and a co-lead, because few of these VC guys want to go it alone. It's all about spreading the risk. After careful consideration, I decided on Walden as my lead, and I told them to take a close look at 3i. "I like them because they have experience in Europe, and I'm looking to expand overseas," I said. "Let me know if you think it'll be a good fit."

It turned out to be a perfect fit. In February 2005, we closed a deal for $11.5 million in funding. The next step was to put a board together. When you raise money, you have to create a governing board that the investors approve of. In this case, in order to secure the funding, I let the investors handpick two of the board members. The third one came from within the industry, and we picked him together, and the fourth was an outsider, a guy I picked myself. I was the fifth and final board member as well as the company chairman.

I liked all the guys except one, who turned out to be the self-appointed bulldog. If I told you we had a tumultuous relationship from the start, I'd be understating the case. Almost from the very first day, he made no secret of the fact that he thought I was too young to be running such a large company, and he was determined to remove me as CEO. He never stopped to consider that this wasn't my first company or that BlueLithium existed only because I had created it.

For the next year, he kept trying to replace me, despite the fact that the company was humming along, growing by leaps and bounds, *under my leadership and direction*. I remember one night in particular: The board met at my place, in Santana Row, with a view toward going to dinner together right after the meeting. When everyone was settled in, I started my PowerPoint presentation, and the first slide came up: "Presented by Gurbaksh Chahal / CEO and Chairman."

Suddenly the bulldog stopped me, wanting to know when I'd become chairman. I looked over at him, incredulous. The guy had been on the board since almost the beginning, and just about every packet that got sent out listed me as CEO and chairman. Then I realized he had done this deliberately, that he was engaging in a form of psychological warfare.

I suspect he wanted me to behave erratically in front of the other board members because he was still determined to find some way of replacing me. I took a deep breath and smiled tightly. "Let's get this show on the road, okay?" I said. "I'm hungry."

He sat through the presentation without saying another word, and he said nothing to me during dinner, but on our way out of the restaurant he couldn't resist a little dig: "You know, G, BlueLithium is growing faster than you are. You're going to need some help. Maybe you should think about hiring some senior people."

I didn't respond immediately. I knew what he was after. He was looking for me to hire someone who might eventually replace me. The other guys on the board didn't seem as eager to push me aside, and I liked them well enough. They were smart, accomplished men, slow to make decisions at times, and certainly a little old-fashioned about business, but otherwise I couldn't complain. And the fact is, if you looked at it from their point of view, maybe I *was* the problem. I was impatient. I liked getting my way. And I was quick to show my displeasure. I began to long for the old days, when I ran the show as I saw fit. I missed being a dictator.

Still, I can handle criticism. In fact, I welcome it. I think criticism is the best form of discipline because it makes you look at yourself. At the end of the day, it tests your maturity, your wisdom, and your ability to make the right decisions. But none of this felt like criticism; it felt more like an attack—and there's nothing constructive about attacks. This wasn't about my management skills or about helping me become a better version of myself but about pushing my buttons.

By this time, mid-2005, BlueLithium had moved twice, and each office was bigger than the preceding one. Nothing too fancy, though; nothing too expensive. We moved because we were growing and because we needed the space, not because we were trying to impress anyone.

We were also busy opening offices across the country. At that point, we had branches in San Francisco, Los Angeles, Chicago, Atlanta, New York, and Boston, and I had my heart set on opening an office in London. I began to look into the possibility, and I found two or three promising candidates overseas, all of them high-priced rock stars, but that part of it didn't bother me at all. As I had learned long ago, you can be cheap about furnishings, but you can never be cheap about people.

In late December, as I was narrowing my search for the right rock star, I heard from ValueClick again. It had filed another lawsuit, this time in the state of New York, claiming that I had hired one of its former salespeople to steal information that would benefit my company. Again, nothing could be further from the truth, but—as I knew from experience—the truth is often the least of it.

Two days later, having given myself time to calm down, I parked myself in front of my computer and wrote an e-mail to everyone on the board, explaining the ValueClick situation. Typically, a board drifts in and out of meetings throughout the year, playing a semi-passive role, but when the shit hits the fan, they're expected to be there to support their CEO. The lawsuit wasn't going to make anyone happy, of course, but I had some news that I felt would soften the blow, and I included it in my e-mail: We had had a record month, I wrote. In the space of thirty days, BlueLithium had *tripled* its revenues. This was truly unheard of. If you are part of a company that registers that kind of growth, in that short a time, you have every right to be ecstatic. Amazingly, I didn't hear back from any of the guys on the board. Not about the lawsuit, and

not about our unparalleled growth. It was as if they were pun-
ishing me with their silence.

Finally, shortly after the New Year, I heard from *one* of
the board members and I just exploded. "What is going on
with you guys? The one time I need you, you're not there!"

"G—"

"At the very least, this B.S. lawsuit notwithstanding, you
can say you appreciate what I'm doing for this company. You
invested in it. Every dollar I bring in puts money into the
pockets of our investors and shareholders."

"G, hear me out for a minute!"

"I'm listening!"

"At a time like this, the board has to take a step back to try
to figure out exactly what is going on. As soon as the attorneys
tell us that you haven't done anything wrong, we'll all breathe
a little easier."

"So you won't even give me the benefit of the doubt?"

"That's not the point."

"Yes, it is," I shot back. "I'm innocent until proven guilty.
Last time I looked, that's the way it works in this country."

Over the course of the next couple of weeks, the attorneys analyzed everything on my computers and interviewed
everyone involved. This internal investigation didn't worry
me, however, because there was nothing to discover—and

nothing *was* discovered. But I was still angry with my board, and a huge wall went up between us. I was on one side, they were on the other.

Still, if I looked at it *objectively*, I saw their point. They needed to be sure that I'd done nothing wrong, and if this is what it took, I would live with it. That was the process. There was nothing to prove. And once it was over, they would realize they should have had my back from the start. When all was said and done, I knew I would come out of this looking better than ever.

> **Good lesson here: If you've got nothing to hide—and you should *never* have anything to hide—don't sweat the process.**

Instead of obsessing, however, I tended to business, and later that same month I opened an office in London, hiring one of the top guys in the country. He didn't come cheap, and the board immediately attacked me for it, so I had to take the time to explain why it was critical to have a rock star on the team. They weren't convinced, but I refused to back down, and within a year we had become the second largest ad network in the United Kingdom. Not counting the bull-dog, everyone on the board was very pleased—and they actually went out of their way to tell me so. I began to feel that the wall had finally come down and that we were again operating as a team. I was young, and I was impatient, and I had made my share of mistakes, but everything I did was designed to take the company into the stratosphere and I thought they were beginning to see that.

Meanwhile, as the battle with ValueClick continued to rage, I went out and hired a chief financial officer, Bill Lonergan, with whom I connected immediately. We had immense trust and respect for one another. What's more, despite the fact that he reported to me I genuinely looked up to him as my true right-hand man. And it truly is a small world because he actually knew Sam Paisley, who was part of the brass at ValueClick. I was relying on his knowledge and insight to get us through the mess. "G," he said, "these guys hate you because you sued them for securities fraud."

"I thought that was old news," I said. "I thought that was behind us."

"No. They want blood. They've got you spending serious money in legal fees on a case that has no merit, and at the rate we're going it'll be at least a year before we go to trial."

"We'll win," I said.

"At what price?" he said.

I did the math. He had just told me that I was going to waste valuable time, and potentially millions of dollars, *just to get to court.* "What do you suggest?" I asked.

"Let me go down there and see if I can make a deal with these guys. That's what they really want. They know the case has no merit, and *I* know it has no merit: I did my due diligence before I took this job."

I went to the board and told them what Bill had suggested, and for once we all actually agreed on something. We settled for a large sum, which I am not at liberty to disclose. In the end, however, it was the right move. I had read Sun Tzu's *Art of War:* "He who knows when he can fight, and when he cannot, will be victorious."

In July, eager to get away from all the madness, I decided to take my whole family on a short vacation. We went to Puerto Vallarta, Mexico, hung out on the beach, ate well, and drank too many margaritas. Most important, however, I got to spend time with my nephews and my niece. I wanted them to know me as an uncle, not only as a type A businessman. I tried really hard not to reach for my ever-buzzing BlackBerry, and there were times when I almost succeeded.

A couple of months later, back in San Jose, we launched the new behavioral technology. We hadn't invented it, and we weren't the only people who had it, but I knew we were going to make it work better than anyone else. And I was right. As soon as we were up and running, this key element changed everything. BlueLithium went from an intermediary working with performance-based advertising—the consumer clicks, you pay—to a company that was able to use people's history to target them more effectively. Hence our pitch: *Data is the difference.*

And let me repeat: This was not Big Brother territory. We only had data related to an individual's viewing history in the form of "cookies." If you clicked on Porsches, for example, we could, conceivably, put that Porsche ad in front of your eyes regardless of where you were on the Internet. And while some people might see this as a negative—ads following you around the Internet!—I had another take entirely: I felt, and still feel, that the technology had the potential to make the Web a more pleasant and personal experience. We were focusing only on the ads you might respond to, determined to remove all that random clutter from your screen. Look at it this way: If you don't need a mortgage, and you haven't been looking for a loan, why should you be subjected to that tiny dancing fool that keeps promising you better-than-ever rates?

At the end of the day, and in the parlance of the industry, BlueLithium was at the forefront of *audience targeting based on consumer interest.* In basic English, we were looking for ways to sell you stuff we knew you kinda, sorta wanted. Or, if you didn't want it, it was definitely of interest.

That was key. That's what made us more sophisticated than the next guy. Click Agents was basically a recording system. It tracked clicks. But BlueLithium was into custom segmentation, a *benign* form of profiling based on a person's Internet habits. Everything about the technology was more sophisticated, more robust, way cooler, and way more *accurate*. And it worked like a dream: People were responding to the targeted ads at ever-greater numbers. And the advertisers were thrilled, of course. In essence, advertising is about getting the right message to the right person in the right way at the right moment, and that's exactly what BlueLithium was doing.

A few months later, we were named Top Innovator of the Year by *AlwaysOn*, a technology publication. And that same year a leading business magazine placed us among the top 100 private companies in America.

In late February 2007, there was a lot of consolidation in the marketplace, and we began to see a slate of industry mergers. DoubleClick was bought by Google for $3.1 billion. aQuantive got bought out by Microsoft for $6 billion. 24/7 Real Media was bought by the WPP Group for $650 million.

It felt a little like a game of musical chairs, with one less chair on the floor every time the song ended. And the songs were playing fast. I went to my board and told them that we needed to hire a banker and start a market check. This is a fancy way of saying that I wanted to explore the possibility of

*In 2006, BlueLithium was named Innovator of the Year by AlwaysOn.*

selling BlueLithium. They didn't agree. They thought we should focus on the company's strategic plans.

"Guys, look at what's going on!" I said. "At the very least, we need to test the waters."

In all honesty, I wasn't sure whether I should be thinking about selling the company. We were more than viable—we were hugely profitable, in fact—but it made good sense to test the rapidly consolidating marketplace. If and when the music ended, I wanted to make sure there'd be a chair at the table for BlueLithium.

In April 2007, a month after we had become the second largest ad network in the United Kingdom, we opened an office in Paris. At that point, we had close to 150 employees worldwide, and we were looking more attractive every day. The board knew this, and they finally decided that I was right to at least *think* about selling. We still weren't for sale, but if someone made inquiries about buying the company, we had to be ready for them, so we prepared for a SOX compliance. ("SOX" is short for the Sarbanes-Oxley Act, which was passed in 2002 following several major accounting scandals in the corporate world—Enron, Tyco International, Peregrine Systems, Adelphia—and it is designed to oversee a public company's accounting and auditing practices.) This would help ensure that we had all the necessary controls in place to become a public company, and it would pave the way for a possible IPO—if it actually came to that.

At that point, with things moving pretty quickly, the board thought it would be a good idea to hire a vice president of corporate development. In a larger company, that person's job is to evaluate other companies, to determine whether they're worth buying, but in a smaller company—one like BlueLithium—he or she is there to help map out a strategy for going public. The roles are slightly different, based on the size of the company, but the title is universal.

I hired a corporate recruiter to help me with the search, and he put together a list of possible candidates. Some of them worked for small, local companies, and others were employed by some of the biggest players in the Internet business. I reviewed the list, we narrowed it down to ten candidates, and I sent the recruiter off to do his job. Very early in the process he called with some interesting news: One of the potential candidates had heard very good things about BlueLithium, and—

while he wasn't interested in leaving his current job—he wondered if he might meet with the CEO to discuss other possibilities. I had a feeling this guy was going to broach the idea of buying BlueLithium, and I wasn't wrong. As soon as we sat down together, he asked if we were for sale, and I told him the truth: "No. But if you're genuinely interested, send me an e-mail to that effect, and I'll take it to my board."

The e-mail arrived the next day, and I immediately took it to the board. "Hey," I said. "We're getting interest. Obviously this is the right time to start a process."

Within a week, we hired an investment bank to help us with the market check, and things got very crazy very fast. The bank contacted other potential buyers, and a number of parties expressed serious interest. Finally, on September 4, 2007, after weighing our options, we decided that Yahoo! was the best fit, both from a financial point of view and from the perspective of the company's almost 200 employees. Yahoo! agreed to buy BlueLithium for $300 million in cash.

As soon as I got the news, I sat down and wrote an e-mail to everyone on our staff:

From:     Chahal, Gurbaksh
Sent:     Tuesday, September 04, 2007 4:02 PM
To:       Everyone
Subject:  A Special Day in BlueLithium History . . .

BL Friends and Colleagues:

Seconds ago, we announced the most important development in our history. BlueLithium has agreed to be acquired by Yahoo!!

This acquisition reflects Yahoo!'s deep commitment to being the leader in online advertising. We are pleased and proud to become part of that effort.

I want to assure you that it will be business as usual at BlueLithium. Longer term, we'll work with Yahoo! management to leverage the strong synergies between BlueLithium and the assets of Yahoo! The Yahoo! senior management team shares our belief that the combination of these great companies with the talent, technology and experience we possess will be an unmatched asset to our customers and partners.

I want to personally thank each of you on the outstanding work you've done to get us here. Yahoo! could have chosen to acquire virtually any company in our space. They looked at our competitors, but decided that BlueLithium was the best choice. This speaks volumes about the quality of the team we've built and the passion we've demonstrated over the past four years to be the very best.

In my eyes, being acquired by the #1 Web property in the world is the best possible outcome for BlueLithium.

The deal will have several immediate benefits for us and our clients:

- By combining BlueLithium's advertisers and publishers with the inventory available on Yahoo! and all of its strategic partners, we will bring to market what we believe to be the largest online ad network.
- Gives us access to more and better Yahoo! inventory & pricing.
- Provides additional resources to implement out best of breed targeting technology.
- Gives us access to more Fortune 500 advertisers and brand name campaigns for publishers.
- Yahoo! is a great company to work for. This will become clear once you see all the opportunities and benefits Yahoo! provides.

Finally, the mergers that have taken place this year have reshaped the marketplace. With Google/DoubleClick teaming up, MSFT and AQNT, AOL with Tacoda and Ad.com, it became imperative for us to have that same scale and leverage. We needed a partner the size of Yahoo! to let us continue growing and to deliver maximum value to our employees, our customers and our shareholders.

I'm enclosing a copy of the press release that just went out. There'll be a special All-Hands at 8:30 A.M. tomorrow to provide more detail and answer your questions.

Immediately following the All-Hands, those of us in the Bay Area will be traveling as a group to Yahoo! for a welcome session with Yahoo! senior management. The session is going to be video cast live to BL and Yahoo! employees around the world. Those of you in New York, London and Paris will either be receiving visits from Yahoo! HR or will be traveling to your local Yahoo! office for the video cast. The Chicago and Boston teams will be able to watch the video cast from your home offices.

Following the visit to Yahoo!, there'll be breakout meetings with your department head to discuss details of the acquisition that are specific to your team.

Once again, congratulations to everybody. This is the day we've waited for.

I am very grateful to all of you. To have managed two back-to-back business successes at the age of twenty-five makes me feel like the luckiest man on the planet.

G

It was the first time I had publicly acknowledged my youth, and it was incredibly liberating. I had always worried that people would question my abilities because I was so young, and, indeed, this had happened from time to time ("You know, G, BlueLithium is growing faster than you are"), but now I didn't have to hide anymore. I could be who I was.

My youth didn't seem to bother Yahoo! As part of the deal, they wanted me to remain with the company for three years, and I agreed only because I figured I'd be able to renegotiate the terms before we actually hammered out the contract. By this point, it became apparent—to me, anyway—that

*The BlueLithium team at the offices of Yahoo! on merger day, 2007.*

I didn't do my best work within a corporate environment. My strength was as an entrepreneur, and as soon as this deal closed, I intended to get back to doing what I did best.

When Yahoo! sent over the term sheet, I took a close look, and everything was in there. We had agreed on a price. We had discussed the retention pool (how many of the employees would keep their jobs). We had reviewed the closing conditions. And of course I was expected to continue running the company for the next three years.

I was flattered—Yahoo! felt I was instrumental to the operation—but I was hoping no one would hold me to it. When it came time for the integration talks, an eight-week process, I was actually able to convince them that their own executive sponsor could do an equally good job. I agreed to stay on for four months, however, to help with the transition, and I also agreed to a three-year noncompete agreement. The lesson here is simple: Know what you're good at, and keep doing it. In order to succeed, you have to love what you do, so make sure you wake up every morning looking forward to the day ahead.

The deal closed on October 15, 2007, and everyone was very happy. This was not simply a good deal for me but a good deal for every single person at BlueLithium, including the members of my board.

To my great relief, my friend Krishna did very well for himself. As I mentioned, his parents had been very unhappy with me when he left medical school to join BlueLithium, but the day after the deal closed I got a call from his father. "When my son decided not to become a doctor, he broke my heart," he said. "But now I see that going to work for you was one of the smartest moves of his life."

The Ad Revolver team also made out pretty well. At one point, as you might remember, they had almost settled for $500,000, but they ended up walking away with a lot more—enough to retire, in fact—they didn't retire, though. They are still working as hard as ever and that's the lesson here: Success comes to those who aren't only in it for the money.

Everything about the deal felt great.

The day I sold BlueLithium, everyone in the San Jose office went downstairs to a bar to celebrate, and my father came as well. He took me aside and told me how proud he was, but he said he was also a little ashamed. "You became the true patriarch of this family," he told me, and tears sprang to his eyes. "You did the job I was supposed to do."

"You're wrong," I said. "When I was sixteen, and I asked you to let me drop out of school to pursue my dream, you believed in me. It was your faith in me that gave me the courage to do this."

I was almost in tears myself. My father was not an emotional man, and he'd never been generous with compliments.

*G with the pilot of a private jet celebrating the Yahoo! merger.*

I never imagined that one day I would hear these words, and I was very proud. I finally realized how hard he had struggled to make it, and how vulnerable he felt. "You know why this wonderful thing has happened for our family?" I said. "Because of you. Because you taught me that one must never give up. Even when you were at your lowest, you picked yourself up and kept fighting."

Later that week, I took my brother and several friends and colleagues to Las Vegas, to get crazy, to be a kid again, and over Thanksgiving, I went back, this time with my family. We stayed at the Wynn, in terrific suites, and one night I took my father clubbing. By this time I was a regular in Vegas, getting the VIP treatment, and I couldn't tell whether people were staring because I had the best table in the house or because my father—with his turban and full beard—was a peculiar sight in this environment. Perhaps it was a combination of the two.

My father had never been in a club in his life, and watching him was half the fun. He didn't know what to make of me on the dance floor, or of the gorgeous young women in their too-short skirts, and hours later, on our way back to the suite, he turned to me and said. "Well, you're young, and you're single, and I'm not sure what that was all about, but do me a favor: Don't tell me."

I thought that was pretty funny.

# The Secret Millionaire 6

**F**ollowing the sale of BlueLithium, it was business as usual for a few months. Per the agreement, I was there to make sure BlueLithium was integrated into the Yahoo! operation as seamlessly as possible, so I was in the office five days a week, making that happen. But it wasn't all business. Another chapter in my life was about to come to a close, and I was eager to explore new worlds. In fact, I had several ideas for television shows based on my experiences as an entrepreneur.

Meanwhile, as a result of all the publicity over the sale of BlueLithium, I agreed to do an interview with the Fox Business Network—my first live interview. As the day drew closer, I remembered how terrified I'd been when I faced the cameras during that audition for *The Apprentice*, and I began to worry. Still, I was flattered to have been asked, and I'd already given them my word, and when I make a commitment to something—anything—I don't back down.

The night before the interview I had so much trouble falling asleep that I took an Ambien tablet, but it didn't work. I was up till 4 A.M., dozed off for a couple of hours, and by 6:30 I was in the gym, working out and bracing myself for the worst.

When I arrived at the studio, I found out that I was going to be interviewed by David Asman and Liz Claman, two anchors whom I had watched religiously when I first became interested in the business world. Suddenly I was sweating bullets. I was in the green room, waiting, and I tried to calm myself down by calling family and friends, but it only made things worse.

"God, I hope I don't embarrass myself," I told Kamal.

*G being interviewed by CNBC at BlueLithium headquarters (2008).*

"Embarrass yourself? You're not auditioning for anything."

"Except the rest of my life!" I said.

A production assistant appeared, put a mike on me, and led me to the set. I exchanged brief hellos with the anchors, slipped into my chair, and before I knew it the cameras were rolling. The very first question was about the $300 million, and it really threw me: "Your cut of that was how much?"

I felt as if I were being deposed. There was no way to win. If I didn't answer, I was hiding something; and if I did answer, I was revealing too much. I opted for the latter. "A little over a hundred," I said.

The rest of the interview went more smoothly. I focused on their questions and answered them as clearly and succinctly as possible, and before long I forgot that the cameras were even there. Another lesson learned: If you find yourself being interviewed on live television, forget the cameras and focus on your hosts. The rest of the world doesn't exist. It's easier than you might imagine.

On my way home, my cell phone didn't stop ringing. Everyone was calling to tell me how well I'd done. I know they were exaggerating, but I didn't mind. I knew I would do better the next time. I had faith.

I couldn't have been that bad, though, because suddenly I was getting interview requests from other shows. I did a one-on-one with Fox's Neil Cavuto. I appeared on NBC's *Tech-*

*Now.* And I was interviewed by CNBC's *High Net Worth.* And with every time at bat, I began learning the art of the sound byte: "I'm just glad my parents supported me when I dropped out." "Even if I failed with my first company, I knew that that would only teach me how to be successful." "Failure is not an option. You need to pick yourself up, figure out what you did wrong, and move forward." "If it's the right decision, if you feel it in your gut, take the risk. I'm a big believer in risk."

Prior to those appearances, I had been a guest speaker at a number of conferences—Red Herring, J.P. Morgan, Bear Stearns, Ad Tech, and so on—but nothing really prepares you for the adrenaline-pumping experience of live TV, or for the gut-churning bout of nerves that strikes just before the cameras begin to roll. But I don't mean that in a bad way: I actually found myself enjoying it—so much so, in fact, that I decided to explore some possibilities in Hollywood. I was intrigued by reality television, and I'd been thinking about business-themed shows, so I scheduled meetings with three Los Angeles talent agencies. When I flew down for my back-to-back meetings, things didn't go precisely as I'd hoped. The first group of agents didn't respond to my first pitch, saying there had already been shows like it on the air, none of them successful, and they wondered if I might want to consider acting, which was not something that interested me. The second group wanted to turn me into a soap opera star, but that didn't interest me either. The third agency, however, the William Morris Agency, seemed receptive to my ideas, and we also clicked on a personal level. I filled them in on my history, and then we talked in some detail about the process of putting a show together. They discussed the concept of "packaging," and about finding the right "elements" to make it happen.

I didn't know anything about show business, but it all sounded very promising, and I was more intrigued than ever.

Just as the meeting was about to end, one of the agents said he would be remiss if he didn't mention *The Secret Millionaire*, a British reality show that Fox intended to remake for American audiences. "Basically, they're taking a handful of millionaires, guys like you, and putting them undercover in a wholly new environment," he explained. "The idea is for the millionaire to find two or three people that he or she wants to help financially, and of course it all happens on camera. Is this something you might want to do?"

"I need to know more about it," I said. "But I'm definitely interested."

"Well, we're in the business of *generating* money for our clients," the agent said, and he was smiling apologetically. "So this is a little backward: We'd be putting you in a position where you have to give money away."

"I'm not worried about that part of it," I said. "Philanthropy is definitely in the cards."

A week later, I was back in Los Angeles for a meeting with the producer of *The Secret Millionaire*, and he brought a casting director and a cameraman with him. They asked if they could film our conversation, and I didn't object, but, again, the questions were strangely personal.

"What is the most romantic thing you've ever done?"

"I flew a girl to Paris, Vegas, on Valentine's Day, because I couldn't get away from work to go to the real Paris."

"When was the last time you cried?"

"At my sister's wedding."

"What's the best thing about being rich?"

"Freedom."

An hour later, when the camera stopped rolling, they asked me if I would be willing to audition for their show.

"I thought I just did," I said, smiling.

"You're right—you did," they said. "But we're asking you to take it to the next step."

When I got back to San Jose, I went to straight to my parents' place and told them all about it. "It looks like I'm going to be on a TV show," I said. "It's not locked in, but if I make it though the next step of the audition process, it's a 'definite maybe.'" (This last phrase was something I'd picked up from one of the producers.)

*Gurbaksh's mother and father in 2008.*

"Who's going to interview you?" my father asked.

"No, no, no," I replied. "It's not like that. It's not an interview. It's an actual show, where I go to some neighborhood where nobody knows me, and nobody knows I'm a millionaire, and I get acquainted with some of the people, and I try to find one or two of them to help out."

"You mean you're going to give them money?" my mother asked.

"Yes."

"You will help out complete strangers?"

"That's the idea."

"How will you know who to help?"

"That's part of the challenge," I said. "That's what I like about the show."

"But I don't understand," my father said. "Who are these people?"

"Don't worry about it," I said. "It might not even happen. I probably shouldn't have said anything."

"What channel is it on?" my mother asked.

On January 30, 2008, Microsoft made a bid to buy Yahoo! for $44 billion. This spoke to that whole issue of consolidation in the marketplace and to my musical chairs analogy. Microsoft later withdrew its offer, but if a deal had ever materialized, Yahoo! would have been taken out of the picture—and there would have been one less buyer in the game.

In late February, I officially left BlueLithium, and I again wrote my employees to let them know I was moving on. My transitional role was over. And anyway, in my heart I was an entrepreneur, and I knew that—much as I respected and admired

Yahoo!—corporate life was not for me. There's a big difference between running your own company and being a successful executive at a company with 14,000 employees. I knew my strengths, and I was sticking to them.

From:     Gurbaksh Chahal
Sent:     Monday, February 25, 2008 12:57 PM
To:       everyone@bluelithium.com
Subject:  An Incredible Journey . . .

Hello Everyone,

As you know, 4 years ago, I made a very important decision to return to the industry. Today, as my last day, I look back at truly what an incredible team, products, and company we made together. Wow, what an amazing 4 years. I have to say, gladly, that returning to the industry was one of the best decisions I ever made.

We started off 4 years ago with the "Dream Team" with a simple idea of creating a better ad network. 4 years later, we've not only created the best ad network but also the largest global ad network. YOU ALL should be proud for creating this in such a short amount of time!

Every victory has its battles. Through this journey, we faced a lot of obstacles and roadblocks. Having my world-class management team at BL to help solve them was truly a blessing for me.

I'd also like to take this time to thank individually each one of my direct reports:

- Tim Brown, for believing a 23-year-old guy's vision (at the time)—quitting your job at 24/7, successfully executing our vision across the pond, beyond my expectations.
- Bill Lonergan, for being a great true asset to me, working with me on handling every crisis and success with your wealth of experience and knowledge.
- Scott Kauffman, for being a great ally, especially in the board room. :-)

I'd like to also thank the "Dream Team"—you guys are living proof that dreams do come true, twice in a row!

Again, I'd like to thank you all for all of your hard work, discipline, and determination to see BL succeed. Being a part of one of the best brands

*The "dream team" at BlueLithium on the day of their merger with Yahoo!; Gurbaksh with siblings Kamal and Taj in the front.*

and companies in the world was a phenomenal outcome for us all.

As you all know, I will be taking some time off to pursue a list of things I've always wanted to do in life. But, for those of you that know me best, also know I get bored very easily.

Till the next time we cross paths, I wish you all continued success.

Yours truly,
Gurbaksh Chahal
Founder, BlueLithium

Not long after, *The Secret Millionaire* actually went into production, and it was truly an amazing experience. I've always tried to be generous, particularly with my family, but I learned that if you help people out—even complete strangers—it also makes you feel really good about yourself, sort of like a runner's high. So you might say there's an almost selfish component to giving. But that's cool, too. It was clear to me that philanthropy was going to be a big part of my future.

# The Lessons of Entrepreneurship 7

The Secret Millionaire was not scheduled to air until December 2008—the producers were off filming other millionaires, in other situations—and I again found myself talking to the William Morris Agency about potential television shows, most of them revolving around my background as an entrepreneur.

The agency set up a number of meetings for me, and I flew to Los Angeles and discussed my ideas with various producers, some of whom seemed genuinely interested. Since I am not the most patient guy in the world, however, and since I'm not inclined to sit around doing nothing, I decided to start laying the foundations for my next company.

At the time, my noncompete with Yahoo! was still in effect, so I had to steer clear of the advertising business. This was just as well, however, because the advertising business was going a little crazy. Earlier in the year, there had been reports in the press that Google's clicks were going flat, and at one point the value of the company's stock had dropped by more than a third, from $750 a share to $460. Analysts blamed lackluster advertising and a decline in the overall economy.

Then in March, Google's $3.1 billion purchase of DoubleClick finally closed, and the company stock jumped 6 percent on the news. The stock was a long way from its record highs, but Google continued to look for ways to dominate the market for targeted text ads, which was a $40 billion business. It wanted to create a one-stop, full-service shop for any company that wanted to advertise online, and one of its selling points was its ability—not unique, of course—to track viewers and target ads. Again, that's what it was all about: getting the right ads in front of the right eyeballs, based on a person's taste, lifestyle, and viewing history.

Once again, there were a number of stories in the press about the amount of personal data that was being collected by large Web companies and about the potential threats to our privacy, but the reporters were missing the point. It wasn't about information; it was about selling stuff. At the end of the day, it was capitalism, pure and simple.

Still, these were tough times in Silicon Valley. In the first three months of 2008, only five companies backed by venture capital investors had gone public on Wall Street, down from thirty-one companies in the fourth quarter of 2007. And the grim news was getting worse by the day. The mortgage crisis was in full swing. (Eighteen percent of Americans had homes with negative equity!) The price of gas was at record highs. The stock market was poised for yet another massive correction. Inflation was out of control. The dollar kept falling. We were either in the middle of a recession or at the end of a recession, depending on who was telling the story. And the government's so-called economic stimulus plans weren't turning out to be all that stimulating.

When I looked around, I realized that more than anything else, the average American was looking for a break on prices. I began to think about online sales and about creating a Web site that would function as a portal to a new kind of shopping experience. Consumers were looking for deals, they were looking to save money, and I had some ideas about how to do it.

The name of my new company popped into my head full blown: gWallet. I didn't even have to think about it. I'd always been a frugal guy. My intention was to help people pinch pennies the way I pinched pennies, to do it the gWallet way.

In March, I wrote e-mails to every venture capitalist on my Rolodex, letting them know that I was about to launch a third venture and that I might be looking for investors. Every single one of them wrote back with a near-identical message: *Let's meet. When are you available?*

I lined up twenty meetings in the space of two weeks, and it became immediately clear that I'd have no trouble getting funding. But later, when I thought about it, I decided that I should go it alone. If I took on a financial partner, I'd be forced to give away a large chunk of the company—that's the way the game is played, and that's what it's all about. (Remember that $11.5 million in funding I got for BlueLithium, money that was never used? The investors went home with about $100 million after only two and a half years, which was a pretty spectacular return.) I also knew, as any businessman will tell you, that I would be much better off waiting until gWallet was up and running, because at that point I'd be negotiating from a position of strength. I would give away a much smaller share of the company for a comparable investment, the smart way to go.

On May 2, *VentureWire* ran a story about my new company. It quoted me as saying that "gWallet is designed to help mitigate the financial burden of purchasing goods with an easy to use online platform" by helping users find the best Web deals. I noted that it would be several months before the launch, and also that I felt the company had huge potential. If I didn't think it was going to be bigger than BlueLithium, I noted, I wouldn't be pursuing it.

On May 13, while I was thigh-deep in gWallet, *The Hollywood Reporter* announced the coming lineup on the Fox Network, which included *The Secret Millionaire:*

> a new series . . . in which wealthy benefactors go undercover in impoverished neighborhoods. For about 10 days, a multimillionaire meets financially destitute locals and experiences what it's like to live on a meager budget for the first time in their lives. At the show's conclusion, the millionaire reveals his true identity to the community and gives a minimum of $100,000 of his own money to at least one deserving person.
>
> "How often do we see somebody who's homeless on the street and wonder what it would be like to live like that?" Fox president of alternative entertainment Mike Darnell asked. "Whereas the super wealthy are so

detached from that experience. This is a really clever conceit and has a great emotional arc to it."

The show was scheduled for December 2008 and suddenly Hollywood was knocking at my door. Did I want to be on a *Bachelor*-style show? Did I want to be on the celebrity edition of *Are You Smarter than a 5th Grader?* Would I want to do *Dancing with the Stars?*

I got a good laugh out of this last one, and thought back to my interview with Neil Cavuto the previous December. "Here's what I want you to promise me," Cavuto had said. "Do not do *Dancing with the Stars.*"

"I promise," I said.

"I think that's a bad career move," he added.

Career? I thought I already had a career. I am, first and foremost, an entrepreneur. But I am open to anything (except *Dancing with the Stars,* I guess since I wouldn't want to embarrass my family on live television). I think life should be lived at full throttle, and I have no intention of slowing down.

In the summer of 2008, as I explored opportunities in Hollywood, I continued to work on the gWallet business model. The deeper I got into it, the more I thought back to the early days of Click Agents and to everything I'd learned since. I hadn't forgotten a single one of those lessons, and I was applying all of them to this, my latest venture.

Let me walk you through a few of them:

- Listen to your heart. We tend to do well at things we love, so find something you love—or learn to love what you're doing.

- Forget noble motivations. Success comes from wanting to win, so you've got to want it bad—you really need that killer-instinct. At the end of the day, no matter what they say, it's not about how you play the game, but about winning. As American football coach Vince Lombardi reportedly said, "Winning isn't everything. It's the only thing."

- Adjust your attitude. Without the right attitude, you'll never succeed. You have to believe in yourself, often to the point of madness, because until you prove yourself the only people who believe in you are your mom and dad (if you're lucky). If you have any doubts, get out now.

- Figure out what you're good at. Very few of us are gifted, so we need to work with the gifts we have. If you're five-foot-two and you love basketball, let me be the first to tell you: It's probably not going to happen. (But don't let me stop you.)

- Trust your gut. We are complicated creatures. That inexplicable feeling you get sometimes—well, it tends to be right a lot more often than it is wrong. Try not to overanalyze it. Some mysterious Inner You is trying to help by pointing you in the right direction.

- Do your homework. Before you start anything, make sure you know exactly what you're getting into. Ignorance is dangerous. What you *don't* know can and will hurt you.

- Be frugal. The only person you need to impress is yourself, and you'll be impressed by success, not by a sleek office with Giorgio Armani couches. It boils down to need versus luxury, and a fancy office isn't going to improve your performance.

- When it comes to staffing your company, however, *don't* be frugal. Find the right people for the right jobs, and pay them what they're worth. We all love and need rock stars.

- Hire the smartest people you can find. Smart people make beautiful music together. Lots of smart people, working in unison, can have the force and power of a Beethoven symphony.

- Don't expect perfection from yourself or others, but never stop striving for it, and try to inspire others to strive for it too.

- Learn to listen. Everyone has an opinion, and everyone is entitled to an opinion, and even wrong-headed opinions can open your eyes to things you might otherwise have missed. So listen, even to the people you disagree with—and maybe to them more than the others. Then process what you've heard and have the courage of your convictions.

- Own your mistakes. At the end of the day, every decision you make, even if it was inspired by misguided advice, is *your* decision. Nobody wins when you start looking for someone to blame. Let it go. Keep moving. Forward movement is everything.

- Never compromise your morality. We all need to live by a moral code.

- Never lose sight of the competition. While you're playing, someone else is working and catching up, so learn to play with one eye on the competition. You're not going to be on top forever.

- Watch your back. Somebody should make a T-shirt that says: "For every back, there is a knife."

- Don't procrastinate. Procrastination is just another word for wanting to fail. If you're not hungry enough, if you're too lazy to move forward, you're never going to get anywhere.

- Don't do anything by half-measures. Remember: Mediocrity is for losers.

- And speaking of which, take the advice of that late great comedian, Jimmy Durante: "Be nice to people on the way up because you will probably meet them on the way down."

- Always negotiate from a position of strength. If you need something from the other guy, you've already lost. People want what they can't have. Become the thing people want.

- Expect the unexpected. If you're ready for anything, you'll still be unpleasantly surprised—but at least you'll get through it.

- Remember: Perception is reality. What they see is more important than what *is*, so show them what they want to see and tell them what they want to hear. (Read that sentence again. It's really quite simple, and it makes perfect sense.)

- Don't get emotional. Logic and emotions don't mix.

- Be fearless. The road to success is paved with failures. If you're afraid to fail, you'll never succeed.

- Pick your battles. The fighting never really ends. Don't let the meaningless skirmishes sap your strength; you're in this to win the war.

- Grow a thick skin—a *very* thick skin. People will question your ability to succeed, and the loudest among them might make you doubt your own talents, so you'll need a thick skin to drown out the noise. The silence will help you focus on your objective, and you will prevail.

- Take chances. Without risk, there is no reward. But make sure it's *intelligent* risk. Only a fool bets against Tiger Woods (until it's time to bet against Tiger Woods).

- When you commit, you really have to commit. Become unstoppable. And don't quit. As Chinese philosopher Lao Tzu put it, "A journey of a thousand miles begins with a single step."

Success is really about making it happen. It's about dreaming. It's about finding that one thing you love above all others and then figuring out how to do it better than anyone else. Remember, I didn't reinvent the wheel. I simply found something that captured my imagination, and then I figured out how to do it better than the next guy.

Most important, I never stopped believing in myself. Business excited me, and I wanted to be good at it. I wanted to be better at it than anyone else. I wanted to win. And winning is about money, sure—but that's only part of it. To me, winning is about leaping out of bed every morning, excited about the day ahead.

You will have bad days. There will be setbacks. You will have more than your fair share of failures. But at the end of the day, you pick yourself up and keep going. That's the Big Secret of Life.

You fall down, you get up.

I know this to be true because it worked for me, and I'm just a guy like everybody else.

And that's what *The Dream* is all about. It's about reaching for the top without ever compromising your morals. Do the work. Keep your eye on the tiger. Fight like hell. Defy the odds. It's worth it. Some people think success is the best revenge, and they may be right, but for me it's much simpler than that:

Success is its own reward.

*The Chahal family in California (2007).*

# Index

9516 Cross Rd

Perry hall

MD

21128